LEGENDS, LORE & TRUE TALES

— OF THE —

CHATTAHOOCHEE

LEGENDS, LORE & TRUE TALES

OF THE

CHATTAHOOCHEE

MICHELLE SMITH

THE
History
PRESS

Published by The History Press
Charleston, SC 29403
www.historypress.net

All images courtesy of Michelle Smith unless indicated otherwise.

First published 2013

Manufactured in the United States

ISBN 978.1.62619.022.1

Library of Congress CIP data applied for.

To Conner, you will always be my best inspiration.

CONTENTS

CONTENTS

ACKNOWLEDGEMENTS

My stepfather, Steven Price, could weave a story. He once convinced me I could catch a duck by tying a lily pad to my head, breathing out of a straw, swimming under the duck and grabbing its feet. To his surprise, he caught me almost falling into the lake. He had me absolutely convinced that egrets grew on trees and fell off when ripe, flying away to the cattle fields. He never let me live down my gullibility, but I'll never forget those funny little tales. He was just one of the many storytellers in my life.

I had the pleasure of listening to the late Kathryn Tucker Windham. Her *13 Alabama Ghost Stories and Jeffery* paled in comparison to her in-person tales of the little people who lived under her bed with bloody swords, and I still thank her for helping me with my insomnia by teaching me the "shoe trick" so ghosts don't know if you're coming or going.

But one of the best storytellers is my former youth pastor, Judge Frank "Trippy" McGuire, of Opp, Alabama. Trippy would load us kids up in his "Gator Chaser" (big green Suburban), and we would take off on some wild adventure. We went cave exploring and cemetery visiting. He told us stories about Grancer Harrison of Harrison's Graveyard and of the Pea River Wild Woman. He had us squealing and screaming when he stopped over the bridge and rolled down his window to call her name. I still like to contact him about bits and pieces of history from the area.

These great storytellers are my inspiration to pass along the legends and lore of the Chattahoochee Trace. Southeast Alabama and West Georgia are full of such rich history that it seemed a shame not to pass it on with my own little twist. I'd like to thank these storytellers in my life who taught me the real meaning of history and a good time.

I'd like to thank Faith and Tony Serafin and the Alabama Paranormal Research Team for their eyewitness accounts as well as Creepy Mountain Research for its vast knowledge of Bigfoot. An additional thank-you goes to Faith Serafin for helping me get these photos knocked out. Your advice and willingness to help even when you had your own deadlines was always appreciated. I also want to thank Brandon Stoker for your stellar artwork. Your talent is awe inspiring, and I'm so lucky to have the opportunity to share it.

I'd also like to thank many people who I met along the way: Mike McClelland at McClelland's Critters, "Deborah" for the hoodoo story of her mother, the random stranger who told me the story about saving a girl lost on Blood Mountain (I'm still not convinced he wasn't Nunnehi since he wouldn't even tell me his name) and countless museum staff members and park rangers—you were all integral parts of writing this book. I also want to thank all my great history buff friends. Those small bits of history that you managed to find in the dank basement of some old library and wrestled out of the hands of a ghost librarian and passed on to me, that's the stuff I live for.

Most importantly, I'd also like to thank my family for their constant support. I'd like to thank my mom, April Turner, for her great advice. Her literary skills are that of a Jedi. I'd like to thank my sister, Lori Gwaltney, for traveling and taking photos for me when I was on a truncated timetable, and my nieces, Abbe and Gracen, for being dragged along and for the great illustrations they drew of stories in this book. To my husband, Billy Smith, thank you for listening to these stories over and over until I got them just right; I'm so grateful you didn't mind being dragged all over the South to explore these great legends.

Lastly, thank you to my son, Conner Smith, for listening to the tales I told you at bedtime (and for your advice on how they would sound better if they were creepy); our constant travels along the Chattahoochee became some of the greatest memories for me, and you are forever the reason I will be a front-porch talker long after there are front porches.

INTRODUCTION

Storytelling has been around since the beginning of the human race, long before ancient texts were discovered and even longer before books were put into print and publication. Often, stories were told in picture, but more often than not, stories were told by word of mouth to convey a message or to keep a heritage and culture alive.

America did not see written language until European explorers came; yet somehow, the aboriginal peoples, known today as American Indians, kept their cultures alive through use of these tales. Many of the native stories are still alive today, especially in areas that were once specifically Indian territory, such as Alabama and Georgia.

Incidentally, the phrase "American Indian" is a story itself. "Indian" was not used to describe the Native American peoples until Christopher Columbus came to America in 1492. Believing he was in the West Indies, he began calling the natives "Indians."

Along the Chattahoochee, tribal remains have been found of Woodland, Swift Creek, Mississippian, Catawba and some Chickasaw groups. By the time America was established as a sovereign country, Cherokees and Creeks were the most common. Some of the first legends of Alabama and Georgia came from cave drawings of the horned serpent and a large effigy in the shape of an eagle, most likely from the Woodland Indians. Unfortunately, with the introduction of disease and the resulting decimation of the native peoples, tales from the Swift Creek and Woodland periods can only be told through archaeology. Their legends have died out along with their people, a grave reminder of the importance of storytelling.

Firsthand accounts and tales of the woes of war, destruction, death, disease, superstition, evil and magic are just some of the tales told along the Chattahoochee River. The river forms the southern half of the Alabama and Georgia border. Its 430-mile-long waters wind their way to join the Flint and Apalachicola Rivers, making the Apalachicola-Chattahoochee-Flint (ACF) River Basin. The name *chattahoochee* is thought to mean "painted rock" or "rocks marked," probably referring to the colored granite that outlines the river's outcroppings.

The Chattahoochee was known for its great importance to both Indians and Americans for living resources, and during the Civil War, it was one of the last strongholds for the Confederate army against General William Sherman on his March to the Sea. The people who come from the Chattahoochee Trace are known as vibrant and passionate. The "Hooch," as the river is often called, still serves as a main source of commerce and a way of life for many Alabamians and Georgians.

The legendary status of this great river is a tale that deserves to be told, not just as several individual stories but also as an interweaving tale. The aboriginals forged relationships with explorers who became colonists who enslaved Africans and then took the lands from the Native Americans. These three cultures also interweaved. The beliefs of the white man became mixed with African superstition and Native American medicine. The Native Americans intermarried with the whites, taking on more autonomy by living outside the centralized community. Each story cannot be told without the other. From the native hairy men and Bigfoot legends to the history of each culture that occupied the area, the tales of the Chattahoochee are meant to be told.

As I tell these tales to my nieces, son and their friends, I love to see their faces in wide-eyed amazement and know I'm passing on to them the greatest lessons in life, those of history they won't learn in school. As they grow older, I hope they become storytellers as well. These future generations are the ones who believe our legends with the faith of a mustard seed. Their beliefs and imaginations are the pinnacle reason these legends stay alive and why it is important to keep up the tradition of telling our history, be it with legends, lore or true tales.

Part I

CRYPTIDS AND SHAPESHIFTERS

Chapter One

KOLOWA THE HAIRY MAN

Alabama and Georgia Creek Indians are commonly referred to as Muskogee Indians. There are many tribes, such as the Upper Creek and Lower Creek. Before 1836, the original homeland of the Creek Indians was still mapped out as Indian territory and was largely unoccupied by European colonists. Within the territory were six political districts—Coweta, Deep Fork, Eufaula, Muscogee, Okmulgee and Wewoka—which were much like a county or parish is to a state.

The Creeks first contacted Spanish explorer Hernando De Soto in the 1540s. Forging a relationship with outside European settlers, many tribes fought alongside U.S. general Andrew Jackson in the Creek Wars of 1813–14. They even fought against other rival tribes, such as the Red Sticks at Horseshoe Bend in Alabama. Soon after the death of the federal Creek liaison Benjamin Hawkins, President James Madison appointed former Georgia governor David B. Mitchell to be the new agent to the Creeks. Mitchell began to undermine the Creeks' sovereignty and began to take their land away from them, specifically in Georgia. Many of the Creeks left the territory by 1836–38. They traveled along the Trail of Tears to Oklahoma, where they became one of the commonly named "five civilized tribes."

Native Americans name an animal by three main categories: what it looks like, what sounds it makes and what it does. Known to make hoots, howls, grunts, growls and whistles (and also, in rare instances, impressions of a primitive language that sounds much like a woman talking or crying), it isn't surprising the Creek Indians of Alabama and Georgia would call this hairy man Honka.

Kolowa was originally a Crow term for the hairy man. It was later adopted by the Creek.
Art courtesy of Brandon Stoker.

Along with the forced removal of Creek Indians came changes to their culture. Mixture with other tribes for survival also led to changes in their legends. Many Creek tribes adopted the Crow Indian term *Kolowa* for the hairy man. The following is a Creek derivative of the Kolowa story. "Lodge Boy and Thrown Away" is a popular Creek story about two young boys who battle the Kolowa. There are many other tales of the boys battling the Kolowa as great warriors. This particular tale was often told to children in the tribes to keep them from running off or being hurt.

A hunter, who had been in the forest for many days, shot a deer at last and turned toward home with his prize. His lodge stood apart from the village, close to the woods, and when he came near, he called out, "Wife, is the cook-fire ready?" But his wife did not answer. He looked for her but found only spilled baskets of corn, nuts and dried berries—and a newborn baby boy.

After searching for his wife and other villagers, some came out of the woods. They told him Kolowa ate his wife and others in the village. The man's heart was as heavy as stone, for his wife was dear to him. Time passed, and the new son she left behind learned to walk and to talk and to play. Every day he grew dearer to his father. "Stay close to the lodge, and hide if a stranger comes," the father said to the boy each day when he went off to the forest to hunt. He said this because he feared that the monster Kolowa would come back.

One day, the father returned to see another small boy playing with his son. The father watched for a while from behind a bush and saw that the boy looked exactly like his own, except that he was naked and his hair was dusty and tangled. When the hunter moved nearer, the strange boy leapt up and ran away as fast as a rabbit.

The next day was the same. The thrown-away boy came to play with Lodge Boy, but when the hunter returned, Thrown Away ran off into the forest. The hunter's heart leapt up; he had to catch the boy, tame him and raise him as his own. On the third day of trying, the hunter caught Thrown Away and set out to tame him with kindness. The boy learned to call the man "Father," but he grew only half tame. He still liked best to have his own way.

When Lodge Boy and Thrown Away grew old enough, their father taught them to paddle a canoe. Again, he warned them about the monster Kolowa. "If ever the canoe is on your side of the river, and someone on the far side calls for you to come and paddle them across, first be sure that it is I and no other. Go for no one else. It may be a trick of Kolowa, who killed your mother."

"Yes, Father," said Lodge Boy.

The next day, after the hunter went into the woods to hunt, the boys went to play by the river. Soon they heard a voice cry, "Canoe! Canoe!" and they saw an old woman on the far side.

"Come, young warriors!" she cried. "Come paddle me over to your side."

At once, Thrown Away ran to the canoe and took up a paddle. "Come," he called.

"No!" cried Lodge Boy. "Father said we must not go."

Thrown Away was angry. "You will come," he shouted, "or I will go away and never come back."

So Lodge Boy went with him.

When their canoe reached the far bank, the old woman did not move. "It is hard for me to walk," she said. "People always carry me down to the canoe on their backs. I am not heavy, but you are very young. Perhaps you are not strong enough."

"I am strong enough," Thrown Away said loudly, and he sprang from the canoe. Taking the old woman on his back, he carried her down to the river.

"People always keep me on their backs in the canoe," she said. "I am not heavy, but you are very young. Perhaps you cannot carry me and paddle, too."

"I can!" Thrown Away said proudly, and he stepped into the canoe. With the old woman on his back he could not paddle as well as his brother, but still they reached their own side of the river safely.

Thrown Away jumped out and pulled the canoe partway up the bank so that the old woman would not have to step in the water. He lifted the old woman and began to set her on the bank. Then, before he could put her down, she turned shapes and shouted, "Kolowai'l, Kolowai'l!" and held fast to his back.

"Get off!" Thrown Away shouted angrily. He hit at her over his shoulder, and his hand stuck. "Get off!" He hit with his other hand, and that stuck, too. "Get off!" He hit back at her with his head, and that stuck to her. He hopped on one foot and kicked back at her with the other, and when even that stuck, he fell over.

"Get off!" cried Lodge Boy, and he picked up a thick stick to hit at the old woman. That stuck too, so he found another and struck her again. But it fastened itself to her like the other. "Old witch, let go of my brother!" he screamed and beat at her back with both hands so that he was caught, too. Old Kolowa opened her mouth wide to begin eating them, but the boys shouted and wriggled and rolled her around so that she could not take one bite.

While they rolled and wriggled and shouted, the boys' father appeared on the far bank of the river. "Canoe, Canoe!" he called, but no one answered. He saw the boys struggling on the banks with Kolowa, so he jumped in and swam across. When he reached the other side, he stood with his hands on his hips and looked down at the hungry old-woman monster and the two boys.

"I told you so," he said. "I hope you have learned to listen." And then he walked to the lodge, built a cook-fire and cooked his dinner. While he ate, he put a large pot of water on the fire. When it boiled, he carried it to the riverbank and poured it over the old woman.

"Ai-ee!" cried the boys as the hot water melted them off the monster. The old woman shrieked and flew off, crying, "Kolowai'l, Kolowai'l!" And the hunter went back to finish his dinner.

Chapter Two

BIGFOOT

The Creeks were not the only Native Americans who had a term for the hairy man. There are more than sixty terms in Native American culture for this creature. This creature is not just a bedtime-story monster but is also believed to be a real flesh-and-blood being. The hairy man is thought to be a bipedal, nonhuman primate. In American culture today, he is commonly known as "Sasquatch." He is also commonly known by Americans as "Bigfoot," a name dubbed by the media in the 1960s. While still listed by scientists as a cryptid, or a mythical creature, Bigfoot has gained popularity throughout North American culture, especially since the 1967 release of the controversial Patterson-Gimlin film showing a female Bigfoot walking through the woods.

The Bigfoot Field Research Organization, or BFRO, has reported over 60 cases in Alabama since the 1980s and 108 cases in Georgia. Other Bigfoot research teams have also reported over 100 sightings since the early 1900s. One area with frequent sightings is around the Appalachian Trail and down into the Chattahoochee Trace. Lee, Russell, Dale, Covington, Dallas, Henry and Barbour Counties in Alabama and Stewart, Carroll, Douglas, Cobb, Gwinnett, Bartow, Cherokee, Lumpkin, Troup and Fulton Counties in Georgia seem to be the concentrated areas in those states.

The stories told do not show Bigfoot's violence to humans but report a more curious and reclusive primate. Reports often include the biped eating cat food or digging through trash in more populated areas and throwing small pebbles and whistling at campers in the more rural areas; however,

Trees are often bent over or snapped at the center to mark a Bigfoot path or territory.

these creatures have been reported to kill deer, even snatching them right in front of a hunter. They have been known to retain small animals, such as kittens and turtles, as toys or pets. Researchers often state when you leave a gift for Bigfoot, such as food, you often find a small animal or fresh kill in its place, considered to be a gift in return. Some stories do consist of massive roars like a lion, dogs being snatched and eaten, trees being pushed over, large rocks or boulders being thrown and tents being shaken; however, there have not been any reports of a person being injured or killed by a Bigfoot.

According to Creepy Mountain Research, a Bigfoot research team from Sylacauga, Alabama, there are different species of Sasquatch. The one most common in this area is known as the long-snouted Sasquatch, which is often gray in color and is said to have piglike nostrils and a long nose. They are commonly mistaken for werewolves, which is also a common legend in Georgia. (The most famous of these werewolf stories is of Isabella Burt from Talbot County, Georgia, who was known to suffer from lycanthropy, but with her smaller stature, she would never have been mistaken for a Sasquatch.) No matter the tale of Sasquatch, the only variable that seems to change is his name. Today, he is known along the Chattahoochee as the Chattahoochee Cootie, Rood Dude, the Alabama Creek Freak, Georgia Pig Man and the Bardin Booger.

Chapter Three

THE LADY WITH THE
GOLD RING

Bigfoot and werewolves are not the only legends along the Chattahoochee, and in some cases, werewolves and witches tend to go hand-in-hand. Similar stories of such witches have been written in Alabama and Georgia volumes of *The Slave Narratives*, a collection of interviews by the last living ex-slaves in America. Many cultures tell stories about shape-shifting beasts, and they are often considered witches.

Even the Native American cultures have stories of shape-shifters often known as skin-walkers. Particularly in the Navajo culture, skin-walkers are known to take the shape of an animal by wearing a part of that animal, such as a pelt or a foot, on their person. In extreme cases, skin-walkers have been known to take the shape of other people. It is said that skin-walkers can use the shoes, clothes, hair or even saliva of their victims to transform into them or to control their minds and actions. If a person is affected by a skin-walker, that person is thought to be cursed and will usually get sick and can even die. Skin-walkers are very fast and can only be killed by being called out. If a cursed person wants to kill or be rid of a skin-walker, they must say to the skin-walker, "I know you are a skin-walker." The skin-walker then loses his power over that person. A telltale sign that a person is a skin-walker is that if he is injured while in a shape-shifted form, the injury remains when he returns to his original form.

"The Witch with the Gold Ring" can be traced back all the way to Europe, and the tale was later brought to America, often told to African slave children as a scary story to keep them from wandering out late at night or trying to escape. Believing that witches come out at night, slaves were most likely to stay put out of fear more than anything else.

There is also a version told locally along the Chattahoochee. This version can be traced back to folk tales from ex-slaves of the Lee County area, recorded by Preston Klein in *The Slave Narratives*.

Once, there was a mill owner from Salem, Alabama. His mill ran twenty-four hours a day. He always had an overseer to watch over the mill: one for the day, and one for the night.

He and his wife lived on a hill overlooking the mill. Friends were always welcome, and there was always company coming and going. The wife was a pretty woman, plain in clothes and without lavish jewelry. She wore only a gold ring for adornment. The only problem was that she always had a crooked smile, which made people mistrust her, as if she had a secret and knew something she didn't share with anyone else.

As it happened, the mill owner had trouble keeping a night foreman. Somehow, they kept getting killed. They were found in the morning, scratches on their faces and blue as a blueberry, as if the life had been sucked right out of them. After the mill owner had gone through ten foremen, he was resolved to work there by himself, but before the night came, a young preacher came to town and stayed at the mill owner's house.

"I'll work the mill for you," said the preacher. "Oh no, I couldn't put you in danger," said the mill owner. The preacher smiled and said, "All I need is my Bible and a dagger. I'll be fine." After back-and-forth discussion, and begging and pleading by the mill owner's wife, the preacher and mill owner had settled it, and the preacher would go to the mill just after supper.

At the mill, the preacher stoked up a good burning fire and settled in to read his Bible while he listened to the workers in the other building. He began to hear meowing coming from outside. He peered out the window and saw more than a dozen cats. He knew a cat could be considered a devil's familiar, and he was hesitant to open the door. But as he peered out the window and prayed, the fire rose up and made the room so hot that he had no choice but to open the door.

As he opened the door, the cats began to rush around. They ran around his feet and made him fall. As he fell, a black cat with a gold ring around the front left paw reached and scratched his cheek. He hit his head and was in a daze. Suddenly, he found it hard to breathe. He struggled for consciousness and breath. Realizing the cat was sucking the air out of him, he grabbed his dagger, which had fallen out of his pocket, and sliced it through the air, cutting the paw clean off the cat.

Cats are often thought to be the devil's familiars in American folklore. *Photo courtesy of Faith Serafin.*

The cat screamed and ran away, taking the other cats with it. Left behind with the paw was something the preacher never expected: a gold ring.

In the morning, the preacher returned to the mill owner's house. The owner greeted him and welcomed him to the breakfast table. The preacher told him about the cats that had tried to take his breath and cutting off one of their paws. As they sat, waiting on the wife to cook their breakfast, she did not come. Knocking on her door, the mill owner called to her, "Wife, it is time to start the cook-fire, won't you come?" The wife responded that she did not feel well and could not come. The preacher coerced the mill owner to let him look at his wife.

They entered the room and found her in the corner, sweating and shaking, holding a blood-soaked towel over her hand. "Wife, what has happened to you?" the mill owner worried out loud. The wife replied, "I was cutting a ham and cut my hand. I will be OK in the morning." Though the preacher could not see her ring finger under the towel, he asked, "Where is your gold ring? Is it not usually on your finger?"

"It lies in my dresser, so as to not get dirty," said the wife, unsteady and shaky.

"Witch, you lie!" The preacher stood in accusation. The mill owner stood, confused by the tone of the preacher. He asked, "Preacher, why do you throw such slanders at my wife?" The preacher grabbed the blood-soaked towel and threw it down, exposing a bloody stump where the wife's hand should be. The mill owner gasped and started to go to his wife. The preacher stopped him and simply exclaimed, "This is what I cut off the murderess who tried to kill me." At that moment, he threw down not the paw of a cat but the wife's hand, covered in blood, and beside it, he laid a shiny gold ring.

Chapter Four

SPRING VILLA DUNNO

Shape shifting seems to be a common tale, but maybe there was something out there that was more than just a campfire story. Perhaps you saw something with your own two eyes but couldn't explain it. You know it's real because people other than you saw it as well. It wasn't like anything you'd seen before, and you pray every night that you don't see it again. This is just the sort of thing that happened at Spring Villa Mansion in Opelika, Alabama.

Spring Villa is a mid-nineteenth-century home built by famous bridge builder and former slave Horace King. It was built for Penne Yonge and his family. In its heyday, this place enjoyed a resort-like atmosphere, filled with steeplechases and glass-bottom boat rides on the thirty-acre, spring-fed lake. Now owned by the City of Opelika, the home, aptly named "Spring Villa Mansion," has been in a slow state of demise with only a caretaker and some ghosts for company. However, this legend lies, not in the haunted home, but on the quartz-rich grounds and surrounding woods that the mansion sits on.

Long before the home was owned by Yonge, it was the home of the Muskogee Creeks. The land was chosen not only for its energy-rich spiritual connection with the Earth but also for its great resources of running water and wildlife. Today, there are still traces of the Creeks. Burial mounds exist on the hillside across the street from the home, and countless arrowheads and other artifacts have been found in the area. But the Creeks were perhaps not the only ones who lived there; there was perhaps something else in those woods, something that might still remain.

Spring Villa Mansion in Opelika, Alabama, was built by Horace King in the late nineteenth century.

Spring Villa Mansion has been the training grounds for the Alabama Paranormal Research Team (APRT) for years. The home and land are known to be riddled with ghostly apparitions of Native Americans in full headdresses and phantom voices of children, and piano music often fills the air even though there is no piano. However, one experience led the team to believe there is something else on the land, something it believed to be flesh and blood and very, very different.

While training one night, several members were sitting on the side porch of the home watching a strange horse and carriage–shaped fog roll in and out. They began to notice the animals in the area would grow eerily quiet as the fog rolled through and then would begin to make noises again as it disappeared. This went on for several minutes, and the group was mesmerized by the strange weather. At this time, a sound came from the wood line in front of the house. A loud and disturbing crash that sounded like a tree falling made many members jump. As they went to investigate, they heard many more thumps, thuds and running sounds through the woods. Whatever it was left even the heavier trees shaking, as if something really big had gone through.

After this strange experience, the Alabama Paranormal Research Team set out to find what it was that could make trees shake like that. Members of the team were aware that black bears had been reported in their county and that panthers were even known to roam in the area, but they also remembered there had been a report made in the Opelika-Beauregard area from January 2000 to the Bigfoot Field Research Organization about a large, hairy and pungent beast that had harassed some boys on a camping trip. APRT members were familiar with not only this case but also such a smell, often commenting on the sweet rotting smell of wet dog around the Spring Villa area. APRT believed Bigfoot could be a reasonable explanation for its experiences, so on September 22, 2012, the group met members of Creepy Mountain Research out of Sylacauga, Alabama, which specializes in cryptic Bigfoot cases, and prepared for a scouting trip at Spring Villa.

They all arrived with equipment and camping gear in tow and set off on a scouting hike during the day. Although there were no finite signs of Bigfoot, there were probable signs. Trees were bent over to mark trails, and some were pushed over across game trails, possibly to trap deer, which are believed to be part of the Bigfoot diet. Footprints large enough to be a Bigfoot's but without enough detail to disseminate were seen in the damp creek bed. The evening progressed, and noise was encouraged. Laughing and roasting hot dogs and marshmallows was one way to draw in any Bigfoot, thought to be a naturally curious creature. The parabolic ear began to pick up sounds in the woods almost immediately, and the teams believed they might be on to something.

Later that evening, three of the women stayed with the fire at the campsite, and the others headed to the field across the street. The women at the campsite became nervous because there were sounds of cackling owls, hooting back and forth in communication, in the woods from all sides. Small pebbles were being thrown toward them as they sat, and strange grunts and twigs snapping resonated from the nearby woods. They left the area to head to the bathrooms and came back to find many things knocked over in the campsite and the noise created by the disturbance caught on parabolic audio.

The team members across the street were standing in the field, observing the wood line with a thermal imagery reader, soon catching a heat signature of something crouched down. The team split up into two smaller groups. One group stayed in the field, and the other went deeper into the woods to track down the crouching object. As the first group observed the second head off into the woods, they noticed what they thought was APRT team member Tony Serafin walk out of the woods, kneel down and stare at them. APRT director Faith Serafin shone her flashlight in his direction, thinking he might have spotted footprints or something. As her flashlight reached the figure they believed to be Tony, they all realized it was not him at all but something else completely. The thing was totally gray but shaped like a man, just like Tony to be exact. The whole team was standing there in a trance-like state, staring at the object, when Tony walked out of the woods and toward them, asking if they had seen it. When he emerged, the creature stood up and walked silently back into the woods, without even a leaf crackling.

The team members were shocked and dismayed. They were going into the woods hoping to see Bigfoot but instead had seen something that they could not even describe. Whatever it was gave them all an uneasy feeling. These people were used to seeing ghosts, but whatever this was seemed flesh and blood, though not human. When a team member was asked what she would call it if she were to name it, she aptly stated, "I'd call it the Dunno, because I dunno what it is, and I dunno if I want to know." What she did know was that nothing good had ever come from that side of the land across from the Spring Villa home.

The last visit they made to the burial grounds was followed by legal troubles, illness and even family members' deaths. They warned against venturing there, remarking that doing so would be followed by trouble and that this strange being could be the reason for that. Faith Serafin stated in her blog about the experience, "We weren't prepared for what we saw, but [we] feel lucky we witnessed it, because we [might] never witness it again. It was very emotional. I understand the paranormal to a great degree, but the experiences we have keep us understanding that we are forever in a learning circle of educating ourselves about what else is here in what we consider to be *our* world as humans, at the top of the food chain; but I'm just not so sure that is the case anymore."

Since renovations have begun on the house, it might not be possible to keep the Dunno a secret for much longer. Many people enjoy the campgrounds that are behind the house, and hidden cache hunts have become popular in the area. It could just be that the secrets of Spring Villa might not stay that way for much longer; all we can do is warn people that some secrets are better left undiscovered and hope the warnings are heeded.

Chapter Five

THE BLACK DOG LEGEND

I t is unclear what the creature is at Spring Villa. What we do know is that it isn't the only otherworldly thing seen in this area. There is another legend known to have an ominous tone, a dire need to cause harm and wreak havoc in people's lives. This legend is known as the black dog.

Sometimes, the dog has been seen on the side of the road by a truck driver just before he crashes. It's also known to run out in front of vehicles, causing them to crash. Sometimes, it has a strange shape. The reporter will at first see a dog, but it will change and look more like a walking trash bag or a black mist. There are a few stories that say this black dog is a shape-shifter, changing form into the dog right before or right after an ominous event. Often, it has been said to fly off, and other times, it just disappears in front of your eyes. Some believe the black dog to be a hellhound, a creature sent straight from the devil to cause trouble among the living.

One particular story comes from an ex-slave named Vannie and her husband, Snipes, both living in Lee County, Alabama, at the time they were interviewed for *The Slave Narratives*. Vannie told the story of the black dog when she was eighty-two:

> *One day, I went to the field early, and a cat was crying and followed me up and down the rows as I worked and cried all day long. We would rock it, and right back it would come, and a boy that was working with us finally said, "I am going to kill that thing." "No, don't kill the poor thing," I said, but someone said, "Something's going to happen," and right then and*

there, that cat just opened up some gray wings, just like a turkey, and said, "Whoof," and up it rose and flew in our chimney....No ma'am, I never seen it no more.

Then, Vannie turned to Snipes and said:

Mr. Snipes, you remember when sister was sick? I sure do. We were sitting around the fire, quiet like; she was birthing her baby, and her lady was sitting there with us and was going to wait on her, [and] I tell you them doors was shut tight, and before God, I saw a figure coming in through that shut door. I punched the other woman and said, "Look yonder, you see that?" She said, "Shut up; you'll kill your sister." Well, I tell you that thing kept coming, and this woman just screamed and tried her best to climb the chimney, [and] I wish you could see her white dress then; it weren't white no more. Well, that black thing just disappeared, and that baby didn't live, not even two months. Later on, I was walking down the road to see a lady, and something kept coming by my side...I never could see it; it just rustled the bushes. I could hear it walking plain as day, but [I] never could find it. Then, all at once came a big black dog, just right out on the ground in front of me, and flapped some old long black ears and flew away. Mr. Snipes knows it's true! Yes, he sure does.

There is another legend of a black dog that comes from the great Creek Nation settlement Tuckabatchee, near what is now Tallassee, Alabama. A large black dog, bigger than a wolf, is often seen gliding along like a mist. He's big enough that you can see him look at you through the window of an SUV. The dog is thought to be a great Indian spirit, possibly the great Shawnee leader Tecumseh. Tecumseh was a major player in the War of 1812, traveling to Creek townships in 1811–12 and recruiting young warriors, such as the Red Sticks, who resisted the white man's way of life. He also played a large part in the Creek Wars, in which Andrew Jackson sought to "clear" Indian populations in Alabama for more American settlers to move in. In his last speech at Tuckabatchee, after meeting resistance to his cause, Tecumseh warned that he would return to Detroit and stomp his foot, and the shaking ground would cause all the houses in Tuckabatchee to fall. Soon after he left, the New Madrid earthquake shook the nation and destroyed many Tuckabatchee settlements in its wake. Many believe Tecumseh set a curse on the town, starting with a comet in 1811 and followed by the dooming earthquakes all around the Creek territory. The curse would ensure that

The black dog is thought to be a messenger of death or bad luck.

Indians who supported American settlers would always suffer and feel uneasy, and the black dog is Tecumseh's spirit, roaming the town, exacting revenge against the white man in any way it can and making certain the curse remains.

No matter its origin, rest assured that if you see the black dog, trouble will soon follow. Some say it is best to pull over, say some prayers and hope the trouble passes you by.

Chapter Six

THE ISTI-PAPA

Another legend involving the Creeks is the Isti-PaPa, a giant, man-eating feline known to roam the countryside devouring livestock and attacking humans. The Isti-PaPa when translated is "lion," but in stories its description resembles a panther or catamount, which make more sense for the area since lions are not indigenous to North America.

One of the more famous stories of the Isti-PaPa states that one particular cat plagued a Creek tribe. Members of the tribe tried to kill it by digging a pit and covering it with a net made of bark. Then they lured it out of its cave by throwing in a rattlesnake. The beast rushed forward with more anger and chased them through the branches. The tribe decided it was better for one to die than all, so the members took a motherless child and threw him before the lion as it came near the pit. The lion rushed at the child and fell into the pit; tribe members jabbed at it with blazing pinewood and killed it. After killing the Isti-PaPa, they took its bones and laid them on either side of the pit. They tarried there seven days because the creature would come every seventh day to terrorize them. In remembrance of the Isti-PaPa, the tribe would fast for six days and begin war on the seventh. If warriors took his bones with them into war, they would have good fortune.

It isn't surprising that the Isti-PaPa has been written about by the aboriginal people of this area. Even still, panthers and cougars are often found near the Chattahoochee, especially in the Wiregrass area of Alabama. Catamounts—also known as cougars, panthers or mountain lions—are tawny brown in color and can weigh up to 120 pounds. There

The Isti-PaPa was known as a bloodthirsty man-eater to the Creek. *Art courtesy of Brandon Stoker.*

have been reported sightings all over the Wiregrass. Today, if you travel to Banks, Alabama—just outside rural Troy, Alabama—and visit McClelland's Critters, you can see several of these majestic creatures. Mike McClelland tells a story about a cougar that he saved from being killed after it jumped from the wood line, snatched a fifteen-hand-high horse by the throat and dragged it back into the woods right in front of its owner's eyes.

Another famous story comes from Panther Creek, just outside Ozark, Alabama. Panther Creek runs just east of Ozark. It was aptly named for the great beast that terrorized the large deer of the area and took meat from the settlers, straight out of their smokehouses. Even in the abundance of wild game, this beast was extraordinarily wild and large. An old poplar tree was found hollowed out several feet deep and wide, and large scratch marks were noted as high as seven feet up. One Saturday in 1830, Curt Byrd, William Andrews, Ben Martin and William and James Martin (brothers) went out for a hunt. They gathered in their primitive vehicles, tooting a trumpet and brandishing their old firelocks, which were polished to perfection, and headed toward the big poplar. The dogs had hooted and howled for about half a mile before they had treed some big game, and Curt Byrd, being swifter of foot, ran to where the dogs were. They greeted him with happy howls. Looking up, he saw a giant beast of a panther, perched and growling, ready to snatch the life right out of whatever was threatening it. Making haste, Byrd raised his rifle and fired. He hit the animal right behind the hind leg. The ferocious beast let out a wild and lofty scream and leapt from its perch to make a break for freedom. It did not get far, falling dead about half a mile away in the woods. The men studied the beast before deciding to skin it and cut down the poplar so that no other panthers could make a home there. The skin measured nine feet from the tip of its nose to the tip of its tail. The pelt went to Curt Byrd, who reveled in his glorious hunt, sharing the skin with all whom he met.

Chapter Seven

THE WAMPUS CAT

Another cat, closely tied to the Isti-PaPa, is the wampus cat. The *ew'ah*, translated as "ugly demon" or "spirit of madness," is a Cherokee Indian legend of a woman-beast hybrid with the ability to drive sanity away. Legend tells that a curious woman wanted to see what her husband did with the elders at night, so she adorned herself with the skin of a large cat and snuck toward the bushes, listening to the old men tell their tales. When she was caught, she was cursed to wear the coat forever, and eventually, her skin joined with the fur and her sanity left. She is still thought to roam the lands, searching for other souls to torture and drive insane. She is also thought to be the eater of children's souls. Throughout the years, the ew'ah began to be called the wampus cat by white settlers and many variations of the tale were spun, especially in the South.

One Alabama legend comes from Old Cahawba, an abandoned town near Selma in Dallas County, Alabama, now listed on the National Register of Historic Places. The wampus cat has plagued the area near the cemetery for years, and some claim it is one of the many reasons the town is now abandoned. The cat has even been so bold as to jump on the hoods of visitors' cars. The visitors' center's tour guide said his sister-in-law and niece were visiting the "new cemetery" area when the wampus cat jumped on the hood of his sister-in-law's car as she went to start it, and the car began to sink into the road, muddy from floodwaters. She tried to start the car but to no avail. After several tries, the wampus cat jumped off the hood and walked back into the wood line. When the coast seemed clear, the mother

The ew'ah, or wampus cat, is thought to be the eater of children's souls. *Art courtesy of Brandon Stoker.*

and daughter jumped right out of the vehicle, running for their lives down the road back to the visitors' center, leaving the car doors open until the next morning, when they went back to retrieve it. They got in, and the vehicle started right up, as if nothing had ever been wrong with it. Cahawba's wampus cat is thought to be the cause of many drowned children on the Alabama River; it lures them to the river with its screams and causes them to jump in with one look of its glowing eyes.

Another Alabama legend says that the wampus cat was created as part of a governmental program in the 1940s and believed to have been crossbred from a panther and a wolf. The U.S. government was thought to have created the animals to be used as messenger animals during World War II, much like pigeons were used in World War I. Something went wrong, and several of the hybrids escaped and bred in the wild. It is now believed that their offspring, the wampus cat, has populated all over Alabama and has even been seen as far north as the Appalachians. Strangely, their populations seem to be heavier near governmental areas, such as Fort Rucker, where large cats are often spotted, and Fort Benning, Georgia.

One man said while hunting with his dog, he came face to face with the wampus cat's glowing eyes and dripping fangs. He heard a howl of desperation and anxiety. He dropped his gun and ran as fast as he could. He heard his dog in the distance, barking and then yelping, yet he still ran. He came to a cabin on the edge of the woods and banged on the door, pleading for help. A man opened the door, and the hunter ran inside, slamming the door right in the face of the wampus cat, causing a big thud. He yelled at the man, "Give me a Bible!" and the man handed him his Bible, which he always kept handy. The man read aloud from the book of Psalms and heard the wampus cat howl and howl until it slowly faded away. He stayed the night with the stranger, for they were both scared to venture out in the dark. The next day, he returned home to find his dog at home in the barn, shaking with fear but alive and unharmed. The man never returned for his gun.

Whether the wampus cat is an experiment gone wrong, a Native American woman or just a case of mistaken identity, we might never know. What is known is that many who have come eye to eye with the wampus cat were either changed by it forever or never found to tell the story.

Chapter Eight

TIE SNAKES AND HORNED SERPENTS

Large cats were not the only animals of unusual size that were mentioned by the Creeks. The tie snake is in several myths and folklore legends written by them, and it is often bested by the Rabbit Trickster, a clever character used by the Creeks to help teach children how to get out of sticky situations.

The tie snake, or *estakwvnayv* (pronounced esta-kwa-nay) in Muscogee Creek, is one of two different snakes in Muscogee folklore, the other being the horned serpent. Tie snakes were the size of regular snakes but with immense strength. They are known to pull fully grown men under water to drown. The horned serpent was much larger, similar to the Loch Ness monster, and was not harmful to man, but it was known for its mystical powers of sight and prophesy. The horns of the serpent were used as medicine. Oftentimes, the tie snake and the horned serpent are mixed together in folklore, thought to be both very large and sinister and still likely to drown their victims. Rock paintings of serpentlike creatures with great horns have been found in many places where the Muscogee dwelled before the Indian Removal Act of 1830. Many believe the tie snake and horned serpent to be freshwater eels, which have been known to drag livestock and men alike down to watery graves.

A common story of the mixture of the two serpents takes place at the Devil's Mouth at Moffit's Mill, a place in rural Lee County, Alabama, often considered home to a giant tie snake that has been the culprit of many drownings. There is also believed to be a tie snake residing in the Chattahoochee River in Columbus, Georgia, which often drowns swimmers and unsuspecting fishermen.

The estakwvnayv, or tie snake, has been thought to live in the Chattahoochee River. *Art courtesy of Brandon Stoker.*

One of the great Creek stories is the "Great King of the Tie Snake," and it paints the creature as a hero:

A chief sent his son to his enemies' camp to deliver a message to their chief of peace as well as give him a canoe as the emblem of the first chief's authority.

The son stopped to play with some boys who were throwing stones into the water. The chief's son threw his canoe on the water, and it sank. He was frightened. He was afraid to go to the neighboring chief without the canoe, and he did not want to return home and tell his father of the loss. He jumped into the stream and dove down at the spot where the canoe had sunk, but he did not resurface. The children returned and told the chief his son had drowned.

When the chief's son was beneath the surface of the stream, the tie snakes captured him, took him into a cave and stated, "Ascend yonder platform." He looked up and saw the King of the tie snakes sitting on a throne of writhing tie snakes. He lifted his foot to ascend, yet the platform ascended with him. Again he tried, and again the snakes rose with his foot. The third time he tried, the tie snakes rose too, and they yelled, "Ascend!" to him. He lifted his foot the fourth time and succeeded in ascending the moving platform, and the king invited him to sit by his side.

"See those feathers? They are yours," said the king to the boy. In the corner, the boy found a plume of feathers and went to reach for them. Three times he tried to grab the feathers, and three times he could not grab them; but on the fourth try, he was able to.

"That tomahawk is yours," said the tie snakes' king.

He went to the place where the tomahawk was lying and reached out his hand to take it but to no avail. It rose by itself every time he raised his hand. He tried four times. On the fourth trial, it remained still, and he succeeded in taking it.

The king said, "You can return to your father after three days. When he asks where you have been, reply, 'I know what I know,' but on no account tell him what you do know. When he needs my aid, walk toward the east and bow three times to the rising sun, and I will be there to help him."

After three days, the tie snake carried him to the spot where he had dived into the stream, lifted him to the surface of the water and placed his lost canoe in his hands. The boy swam to the bank and returned to his father, who was mourning him as dead. His father rejoiced that he was not.

He informed his father of the tie snake king and his message of help. Not long afterward, his father was attacked by his enemies, who had never received the message of peace. He said to his son, "Go and seek aid from the king of the tie snakes."

The son put the feathers on his head, took the tomahawk, went toward the east and bowed three times to the rising sun.

The king of the tie snakes stood before him.

"What do you want?" he said.

"My father needs your help," said the boy.

"Go and tell him not to worry; they may attack, but in the morning, all will be fine."

The son returned to his father and delivered the message of the king of the tie snakes.

The enemy did come. They attacked, but all was well. Night came, and everyone slept. In the morning, when they woke, they found every enemy ensnared by the coils of the tie snakes.

The chief took the time to make peace with his enemies before the snakes released them, and all was well with the chief and the king of the tie snakes.

Chapter Nine

SALEM'S GIANT EAGLES

One of the most interesting stories of animals of unusual size is the recollection of "Uncle" Bert Frederick. Uncle Frederick was interviewed for *The Slave Narratives* between 1936 and 1938. At the time, he was somewhere over eighty years old, and he was living in Opelika, Alabama. Mr. Frederick had had a few different owners as a slave, but as a child, he had belonged to Mr. William Frederick and was known as a "shirt tail." By that, he meant that he only wore an oversized shirt every day and nothing else until he was over twelve years old. Incidentally, Uncle Frederick had a sister named Mary Dowdell. If you have the chance to visit the Robert Trent Jones golf course in Opelika, you will see her grave and possibly Mary herself. She has been spotted there since her death, stealing people's golf balls. Mr. Frederick recollected a story about giant eagles in the area. His job was to drive sheep and cows in the pasture. He also had to protect the calves and small sheep from the eagles. He stated, "Ef us warn't, ol' eagle ud swoop down an' tote off a whole lamb."

Just on the other side of the Chattahoochee from where Uncle Frederick lived, another Indian tribe known as the Cussita made its home. Cussita Indians have a tale of a monster blue bird with a long tail, swifter than an eagle, which began to eat the tribe. They tried to trick the bird by forging an effigy of a woman, hoping it would take it as a mate. The bird came, carried the doll away and stayed gone for a long time. The bird brought the doll back later, and a large red rat crawled out of it. The Cussitas believed the rat was an offspring and asked it how to kill the bird. The rat said the bird

Hawks are more prominent in Salem today, but eagles are making a comeback. *Photo courtesy of Faith Serafin.*

carried a bow and arrow for protection and that he would chew through the bow. Once he did this, the Cussita were able to kill the bird. It is possible this large bird could have been the now-extinct teratorn, which looked similar to a raven. Its wingspan could range up to twenty-four feet wide, and it weighed up to 170 pounds.

Many Native American cultures have a legend of the thunderbird, a bird with magical powers that brings the thunder with it and whose halcyon wings will shine as bright as the sun and whose eyes cause lightning. Thunderbirds are believed to be derived from the North American bald eagle, which has been known to dwarf many other raptors, except for the California condor, which is a vulture. The American bald eagle is thought to be the largest true raptor in North America, closely followed by the golden eagle, whose wingspan can be up to 86.6 inches wide and has been known to weigh up to twenty pounds. While usually going for smaller, easier prey, golden eagles have been known to take deer and even coyotes. Believe it or not, it wouldn't be unheard of for an eagle to swoop down and take cattle. They have even been known to try to take small children, which was also a common tale in Native American lore.

Several different raptors have been known to inhabit areas around the Chattahoochee. Teratorn remains have been found as far south as Florida's banks of the Chattahoochee. Eagles are still common raptors in Alabama, especially the golden and bald eagles. It is uncommon to see bald eagles in the wild today, although they would have been as common as a blackbird in the antebellum South. Bald eagles were often shot as vermin, and when their numbers went down, they were placed on the endangered species list; however, they are making a comeback in the wild after thriving in captivity and are being seen in the Opelika area again.

Part II

THE OCCULT AND OTHER MAGICAL LEGENDS

Chapter Ten

THE DEVIL'S CROSSROADS

Strange creatures aren't the only things you'll find in this area. If you've ever heard the saying, "The devil goes to church and sits on the front row," then you must be from the southern United States. This area, commonly referred to as the "Bible Belt," is full of much superstition and legends of dark, malicious forces. Where there are stories of good, there seem to be more stories of evil. Whether it's voodoo, paganism, hoodoo or Wicca, most people chalk these practices and religions up to plain old devil worshipping and don't bother to learn the logistics. One of the most popular legends is that of the devil's crossroads.

Crossroads are defined as a place where two roads meet or a small, rural community situated at an intersection of two or more roads; however, the social definition of crossroads is a place where an important choice has to be made. And there's no better place to decide whether you'll give your soul to God or sell it to the devil.

Often, it is told that the devil waits at the crossroads for just the right soul to come along. Before the modern urban era, these roads were usually in the center of a field surrounded by a crop, such as corn or cotton. In most of the stories, a person met the devil in the middle of the crossroads to strike a deal or buried an object in the middle of the crossroads as a gift to the devil. The devil then granted some sort of wish in exchange for the person's soul.

The most famous devil's crossroads story is that of Robert Johnson, an American blues singer, who supposedly exchanged his soul to have the devil tune his guitar and play a few songs at the crossroads to make Robert one

Oates's tombstone in Oakwood Cemetery bears a statue of his likeness, accurately missing a hand. *Photo courtesy of Faith Serafin.*

of the greatest blues musicians ever. But with his rise to fame, he seemed to have periods of highs followed by lows, when the devil supposedly collected on his soul. Johnson began to sing about running from the devil, hellhounds coming after him and falling to his knees and crying out for mercy. Johnson died at twenty-seven from unknown circumstances.

It might be possible that the crossroads itself holds all the power. If you were born there, the devil could perhaps decide to have a hand in your life without your knowledge or consent, possibly even make sure you lived a life of uncertainty, violence, infamy and prestige all at the same time. Studying the life of William C. Oates, born at Oates Crossroads in Pike County, Alabama, it makes you wonder.

Born on November 30, 1833, just two weeks after a meteor shower that lasted three days and rained down as many as ten thousand "stars" an hour, William C. Oates seemed destined by the stars to be known. The whole year of 1833 was known as the "year the stars fell," and the event was so moving that it caused church revivals all over the South and fueled the "Second Great Awakening" of religious revival already in full bloom all over the area. People believed it was a sign of something to come, and children born at the time were almost immediately revered or at least looked at as though there were something special about them. The meteor shower would prove to not be the only odd thing in Oates's life. He often offered that his mother was a "prophetess." He claimed she had a second sight and experienced visions. She did not seem to be the only one in Oates Crossroads who had such gifts. This would give rise to many superstitious southerners thinking that this area was marked with the devil's calling card.

As a teenage boy, William visited a neighbors', the Posts, home to see their "spiritual medium" daughter perform a table-raising experiment. Oates leaned on the table, making it rise quite easily. He pointed it out to Post and claimed his daughter as a fraud. Getting in a fight with the father and defending himself, Oates wounded Post in the head. Believing he had killed Post, Oates fled. Post survived but warrants remained.

Like many who claim to have dealt with the devil at the crossroads, trouble seemed to follow Oates everywhere he went, yet somehow, he always came out on top. Joining up with the Confederacy during the Civil War, Oates quickly climbed the ranks to colonel of the Fifteenth Alabama Regiment and was one of the key players at the Battle of Gettysburg. Wounded in battle, Oates returned to the South, and after almost losing his leg, he was invited by Colonel Toney and his wife to stay with them at their home, Roseland, to recover. Flourishing in a lavish lifestyle, full of bureaucratic snobbery, Oates remained there until he was strong enough to rejoin the war efforts. Despite his best efforts, Oates's regiment helped to seal the fate of the Confederacy by being defeated at Gettysburg's Little Round Top.

It seemed his life was a twisting turmoil of success and failures. Losing his right arm while commanding Alabama's Forty-eighth Regiment did not seem to stop him; he used his missing limb as a political "badge of honor" for years to come in his political career in the U.S. Congress. Oates married Sarah Toney, the daughter of Colonel Toney; she was twenty-seven years his minor. There is an old family story that says while Oates was with the Toney family in Eufaula recovering from his leg injury, he was holding infant Sarah in his arms once, when Mrs. Toney said to him, "Who knows, you may be holding your future wife as we speak"—another odd and prophetic twist to his life.

Despite political woes and claims of ballot stuffing and fraud after being elected Alabama governor in 1894, Oates had a long and fulfilling political career, but it left him in deep debt and poor health. Oates tried once more to erect his career when President William McKinley appointed him brigadier general during the Spanish-American War, but the war was over by the time he arrived. It had seemed he had no more political use by 1897. Oates continued a law practice and held the position appointed to him by President Theodore Roosevelt, federal commissioner for locating and marking Confederate graves in the North, until he passed away in Montgomery, Alabama, on September 9, 1910. His tomb at Oakwood Cemetery in Montgomery is inscribed:

> *Born in poverty, reared in adversity, without educational advantages, yet by honest individual effort he obtained a competency and the confidence of his fellow men, while fairly liberal to relatives and the worthy poor.*

Chapter Eleven

THE HOODOO WOMAN
OF TUSKEGEE

The devil is known to be part of a broad spectrum of religions and folklore. His hand stretches far past the biblical Satan and delves deep into many other cultures. The devil at the crossroads also crosses those religious boundaries with the practice of hoodoo. Hoodoo is a nineteenth-century American term and is described as African American folk magic. It is synonymous with conjure, root work, witchcraft and trickery. Contrary to its loose definition, hoodoo has been practiced by both white and black Americans.

Also contrary to common knowledge, the word *hoodoo* can be traced back to the Irish-Gaelic word *uath dubh* (pronounced hooh dooh), which means "dark phantom," "evil entity" and "spiky ghost." The word can be used as a noun, as in "She practices hoodoo," or as a verb, such as "She was hoodooed," meaning someone used magic on the other person. In the nineteenth century, Irish ships that suffered bad voyages or ill fates were known to be hoodooed.

A person who practices hoodoo is known as a hoodoo doctor if male and a hoodoo woman or lady if female. Many of these workers are prominent members of society and travel all over to help their clients. But some prefer to have a more anonymous approach to cut down on any backlash.

While predominantly African folk magic, hoodoo consists of African folkloric practices and beliefs with a considerable mix of Native American botanical knowledge and European folklore. The hoodoo magical tradition does have its own dark deity, commonly known as the "dark man" or "devil,"

The hoodoo woman used the crossroads and a blood sacrifice to add power to her conjure.

and he usually lives at the crossroads. Because of this, "rootwork" is often referred to as "crossroads magic."

Rootwork is the common practice of a hoodoo worker that employs the use of a "mojo bag." Hoodoo attributes magical essences to herbs, minerals, roots, personal possessions and even animal parts. When using a mojo bag, a hoodoo woman will add many of these objects in a pouch to be used by the client against another person for a number of reasons.

If you ask a hoodoo woman if her practice is dark, she will say that it is only as dark as the person who uses it, and that's where the hoodoo woman of Tuskegee comes in. The hoodoo woman of Tuskegee practices anonymously. She doesn't tell people who she is or where she lives. Her services are passed down by word of mouth and are used by a number of different people. The hoodoo woman claims not to be dark or good but gives directions to her clients to do the rootwork themselves so that any backlash comes back on them, not her. She simply tells them how to do it and gives them the ingredients with which to do it.

The story of the hoodoo woman of Tuskegee was told anonymously by a woman named Deborah. She stated if she told the story and revealed certain details of the conjure work, it could become undone, and her mother would become sick again. The woman stated that her mother, Addie, came down with something because she was feeling sick. A woman at church named Lila told Addie she believed that another member of their church congregation had put a conjure on her and she needed to go see the hoodoo woman of Tuskegee. Addie was a God-fearing woman and didn't believe in such nonsense. Lila told her it didn't matter if she believed, the other woman who had laid the conjure on her did. Lila said the only way to get the conjure off was to contact the hoodoo woman of Tuskegee. Addie thought it was silly, but she just couldn't seem to get well. Addie called Lila, and Lila gave her an address of a dirt crossroads in Beauregard, Alabama. She told Addie to go there and bury a letter telling her symptoms and the name of the person who she believed had laid the conjure on her in the center of the road along with an undisclosed amount of money. Lila said to be sure to leave a drop of blood on the ground, drive off and not look back in the mirror once Addie buried the money.

Addie didn't know what to believe, but she was willing to give it a try. So she went to the crossroads and did as Lila instructed. When she woke the next morning, there was a basket on her porch. It had some herbs in it and some instructions. The instructions were as follows:

> *The woman you speak of bought a conjure from me. To undo it, take the roots in the big bag and grind them up into a powder. Put them in your water and drink every bit, don't even spill a drop. Tomorrow, you will go to the bathroom, and something will fall in the toilet. DO NOT LOOK IN THE TOILET! Flush it, and walk away. You will be fine by the next day. To protect yourself further, take the little bag and sprinkle half on the doorsteps to your church and the rest put between your mattresses where you sleep. Don't let anyone touch it or see you do it.*

Addie was worried; she didn't know what the herbs were and thought it foolish to drink something left on her front porch, but she took a chance and drank the herbs; after all, she was very sick, and the doctors didn't know what was wrong with her. To their medical knowledge, there was nothing physically wrong with her, so she had to try this.

The next morning, she went to the bathroom, and sure enough, she heard something fall in the toilet. She flushed it away just as she was told. She put the small bag between her mattresses and went to sleep. The next day, she was feeling better. When she went to church, she sprinkled the herbs. The woman who put the conjure on her went to the steps of the church but did not enter. She took one look at Addie and said, "I will never enter these doors again. I won't share the same space as you." She walked away and never came to that church again.

Deborah said Addie never did use the hoodoo woman again and never found out who she was or where she lived, but she won't remove that little bag of herbs from between her mattresses and made Deborah swear she wouldn't tell what herbs or roots were used or say the name of the woman who laid a conjure on her. Addie says once you say the devil's name, he's sure to appear.

Some people believe Addie could be suffering from *nocebo*, which translates to "I will harm." It is a study that was focused on beginning in the 1960s. Much like its counterpart, the placebo (a medical treatment for which a person is given a dummy pill), the nocebo was used on patients who were told that they had an "illness" that could kill them when, in reality, there was no illness at all. The effects were overwhelmingly in the favor of mind over matter. Anthropologist Robert Hahn of the U.S. Center for Disease Control and Prevention in Atlanta, Georgia, who has studied the nocebo effect, states that a "voodoo death if it exists, might represent an extreme form of the nocebo phenomenon," so it makes sense that the same would be true for hoodoo's rootwork.

Here is an example of how nocebo works. If you say to a person who is perfectly healthy and vibrant, "You look tired. I hope you aren't coming down with something; you know there's a virus going around," he might, in turn, begin to feel tired. His throat might become scratchy, and before you know it, he has come down with a cold. In the same manner, if a hoodoo believer tells you, "Someone has laid a conjure on you," you might immediately feel cursed and sick, even if you aren't a believer in hoodoo.

No one really knows if Addie was sick and cured because of hoodoo or if it was all in her head to begin with. This is such a controversial topic that there have even been movies made on the subject. What we do know is that the belief itself isn't necessary for hoodoo to affect your mindset. Even at the mere suggestion that you are suffering from such folklore magic, you could begin to feel effects. The question that remains is whether Addie's cure worked because she believed or hoped that it would or because hoodoo's rootwork is a new approach to holistic medicine. The truth is, we might never know.

Chapter Twelve

THE GHOST TOWN WATCHERS

There is another crossroads in a small rural area in Lee County called "Ghost Town." On one side of the crossroads is a cemetery and, on the other, several large granite boulders. These crossroads are known to promote strange phenomena, often electrical in nature, and many cars have engine problems or get flat tires. If you travel just down the one part of the crossroads that is dirt, you will find one of the most supernaturally charged places in Lee County. The land is riddled with trees and small dirt trails, large granite boulders and even a makeshift altar that was used many times in sacrifices by local Satan worshippers. Some believe the blood spilled there has scarred the land and made it an unholy place.

Many sightings have been reported by local authorities of a spectral couple, a man and woman, crossing the road and entering the wood line; yet, something else lurks there. Something supernatural in nature, neither good nor evil, something called a "watcher."

There are a few definitions in folklore of a watcher. One is that a watcher is a small being with gray skin and dark black eyes with red pupils; it is usually summoned by a person to watch and report back activity at a specific location. A summoning spell usually includes a small blood sacrifice. These watchers do not interact with anyone except the person who summoned them.

Another definition is a more biblical term. Watchers are from both heaven and hell, and they write down everything that humans do in the book of life. These watchers do not interact with humans at all. They are often thought of as angels and demons. In the book of Enoch, watchers fell from heaven

Watchers are often seen as hooded or cloaked figures.

because they lusted after human women. They married and had offspring, called the nephalim, who were giants with insatiable appetites for both animals and men. The watchers taught the women about things meant to stay in heaven, which is where the occult is supposedly derived from today. When the souls of the nephalim's victims cried out to God, he punished the watchers. Their leader, Azazel, was bound and buried in the desert to stay until the world's end. The nephalim were destroyed and cursed to roam the world as "evil spirits," tormenting both women and children because women sinned with the watchers.

Native American folklore also seems to have watchers of the spirit world. These watchers, also known as spirit people, are often small in size and are very helpful but mischievous. They are invisible unless they want to be seen and can appear their normal size or appear overly large if trying to frighten someone. The Nunnehi, a Cherokee watcher, is known to inhabit the area of Georgia next to the part of the Chattahoochee closest to the Tennessee line. Always friendly, they often help return lost or injured people, especially children, and more than once, they have saved many Cherokee warriors from defeat in war.

So if the watchers don't usually interact with humans, we have to wonder how we know watchers are in Ghost Town. They have been seen and heard, and you can most definitely feel them. The area feels very scary, and there is always a sense of being watched; it is definitely not a place you would want to be alone in, even in the daytime. Often, people report hearing rustling in the woods and glowing eyes peeking out around trees; it is also very common to hear voices in conversation coming from the wood line, yet every effort to find the source is thwarted. One person has reported coming face to face with a group of small beings, each with a single horn coming out of its head. Some believe these watchers were summoned by Satan worshippers through blood sacrifice. Reports of animal sacrifice and even possible murder have been rumored for years in this area. One report even suggests that bodies were dug up to be used in necromancy at this very location.

Because of the negative and malevolent sacrifices that have occurred there, one tends to think these watchers are summoned out of darkness. The area is not to be trifled with. It is patrolled regularly, but signs of human garbage and campfires suggest some of the noises might be people of flesh and blood and definitely suggest it is not a safe area to visit.

Chapter Thirteen

THE DISAPPEARING ANGEL
OF DOTHAN

E vil does not inhabit the earth without a counterbalance of good. An amazing story came out of the Chattahoochee Trace area in the 1990s of what many believe to be an angel, specifically, the archangel Gabriel. In the early '90s, there were several reports coming from people all over the area. Reports from Ino, Enterprise and even Dothan, Alabama, had people believing the world could be ending soon, and a great spiritual awakening was happening all over the southeast section of the state.

Each account was the same. Driving down the road, the driver saw an old man in a baseball cap walking. The driver pulled over and asked if the man needed a ride. The old man got in the back seat. As they continued down the road, the driver asked where the old man was going; the old man replied, "I am the archangel Gabriel, and I'm about to blow my horn." When the driver looked in the rearview mirror or turned around, the old man had disappeared.

In the Bible, Archangel Gabriel is often seen as the exalted messenger of God. Gabriel helped interpret the dreams of the prophet Daniel. He appeared to Zachary and spoke to him about Zachary's son, John the Baptist, and he also came to Mary to tell her about the birth of her son, the savior, Jesus Christ. Additionally, Gabriel is said to be, with a blow of his trumpet, the announcer of the second coming of the Lord in the book of Revelation.

Believed to have a closer connection to the supernatural world, children often tell stories of Gabriel, even when his name is not mentioned in their household. One three-year-old boy told his mother that Gabriel

Angels are said to visit earth in human form.

was responsible for the burning of a building on the campus of Auburn University. When the mother asked who Gabriel was, the boy replied, "God's best friend." Another child, who reportedly had a near-death experience, claimed he had been in heaven and stated that Gabriel sat on the left hand of God, designating Gabriel's status as exalted.

Interestingly enough, there is a city of Dothan spoken of in the Bible as well. The word *Dothan* is written ντδ in the Hebrew pictograph. The first character is a dalet and represents a doorway, gate or path. The next character is a tav, which represents the covenant, and the last character is a seed, which indicates perpetuity. Putting it all together the pictograph translates as "the door or gateway to the eternal covenant." The eternal covenant is known to be the salvation of Jesus Christ. Therefore, Dothan was the "gateway to salvation."

One prominent biblical story that involves Dothan is that of Joseph. Joseph was the son of Jacob (also known as Israel). Joseph's is one of the first stories taught to children in Sunday school, and he is commonly known for his coat of many colors and being sold into slavery in Egypt. As a boy, Joseph was lost while looking for his brothers and was led to Dothan by "a man who found him." Many believe the man was the angel Gabriel in disguise. In Dothan, Joseph was sold into slavery by his brothers. Had Joseph not gone to Dothan, he would not have been sold into slavery; if that had not happened, there might not have been a need for an exodus by the enslaved Israelites from Egypt led by Moses and taken over by Joshua. Many believe without the events, Jesus might not have been born and salvation through his sacrifice might not have been possible. It seemed as if the man who led Joseph to Dothan did it by God's decree so that later God's people, first the Jews and then gentiles, had salvation through Jesus.

Dothan is mentioned one more time in the Bible, in 2 Kings 6:12–19. Elisha was being sought after by the king of Syria. The king sent an army to Dothan where Elisha was staying. Elisha's servant was very afraid as the Syrian army surrounded the home and didn't understand why Elisha was so calm. Then, the servant's eyes were opened, and he saw angels and chariots of fire surrounding them, protecting them from the Syrian army.

Both of these stories have an important celestial connotation to the place of Dothan. Perhaps the fact that Gabriel has been seen in modern times in an American Dothan doesn't seem that coincidental. Since these reports, there have been no other mentions of sightings of Gabriel in Dothan; however, there have been a few reports of other angels visiting the area to help people through tragedy or give a prophetic message of hope.

Part III

GHOSTLY LEGENDS AND OTHER ODD THINGS

Chapter Fourteen

THE LOST TREASURES OF GEORGIA

From lining gleaming celestial streets to legends of its amber glow being produced from the sun, gold has fascinated mankind with a consuming passion from as far back as forty thousand years. The United States is no exception to this rule. In the mid-1820s, a series of gold strikes along the eastern states caused thousands of people with "gold fever" to pour into what is now called the Dahlonega Belt in Georgia, fueling the first American gold rush, unfortunately for the Cherokee Indians who laid claim to that land and the adjacent land along what now is the Chattahoochee Trace.

Ancient Georgian volcano lines were at one time as high as the Himalayan Mountain range. The volcanic activity produced so much gold that it washed down into the valleys as if it were sand. The aboriginal people who lived below had little use for this malleable element, and so it sat on the ground, awaiting European settlers to claim it as currency.

King George of England signed a charter establishing the Georgia colony on April 21, 1732. Between 1732 and 1752, Georgia was referred to as "trustee Georgia" because a board of trustees governed the colony. A council provided a semblance of government from 1752 to 1754, and in 1755, the territory became a crown colony. During the French and Indian War (1754–63), Georgia gave up its claim to what is now Alabama and Mississippi in exchange for a promise from the federal government to remove Indians occupying its remaining land. This cessation was called the Proclamation of 1763.

Indian removal became a priority over the next several years, and helping fuel this fire was the first gold rush in the summer of 1829. Thousands, known as the twenty-niners, poured into Georgia, gold hungry and desperate. Stories were told all over of huge gold nuggets being unearthed. Several stories surfaced claiming the first discovery of the gold-rich location, the most popular being about small Indian boys playing in the Chestatee River and discovering a large nugget. McDuffie County claimed to be the first county to discover gold, one hundred miles south of the main Dahlonega Gold Belt, and even Carroll County had claims of becoming a sort of Klondike, where men came with picks in hand to unearth treasures galore. No matter the story, the land they wanted belonged to the Cherokees, and Georgia was willing to do anything to make the area its own.

The gold rush became known as the "Great Intrusion" to the Cherokees. Despite claims by the federal government to help remove the miners, many of them did not leave. After several arrests of trespassing gold miners on Cherokee land, many of the mines were taken over by the Cherokees. This angered the former miners, and many of them joined a posse of bloodthirsty "Pony Clubs"; much like the later Ku Klux Klan, members of these clubs rode during the night, stealing from and visiting death upon any opponents.

After the Cherokee Removal of 1838, commonly known as the Trail of Tears, the gold rush died out when the land was all but used up, and the twenty-niners began to move west to California, paving the way for the great gold rush of the forty-niners; yet stories remain of hidden gold, buried in caves and underground by the Cherokees.

In Duluth, Georgia, near the junction of what was called "two old Indian trails," sits Craig's Creek along the Chattahoochee River. There was once an old Cherokee village there where anywhere from five to seventy-five pots of gold were reportedly buried. Stories remain that some of the gold was dug up in 1909 by returning descendants from Oklahoma, and some stories say that an old farmer unearthed some pots with his tractor. But many believe that most of the caches are still in the earth, waiting for someone to find them.

Many of the Cherokees were said to have buried gold beneath several creek beds. Scarecorn Creek, Talking Rock Creek and Shallow Rock Bridge Creek were just a few of these. There have even been stories that there is gold buried in the Chattahoochee itself.

The Cherokees were not the only ones who buried treasure in the Chattahoochee. Prior to the fall of Atlanta during the Civil War, a man carrying a pouch of $100,000 in gold coins took a train to the banks of the Chattahoochee near Cobb County. The man marked an *M* and an *X* on a tree and cut off one of the limbs. Just below the tree, he buried the pouch, and then he killed the slave who was helping him carry it. The man gave the

The falls at Unicoi State Park in the Chattahoochee National Forest.

map to his wife shortly after having a stroke, but she searched in vain for it. It would be worth a little more than $500,000 today. The Chattahoochee banks near Bolton, Georgia, are also said to hold treasure that belongs to the Atlanta Bank treasury, and some believe even the Confederate treasury buried up to $2 million in the Chattahoochee River.

Today, gold mining is making a comeback in the Georgia area. Because of the poor economy, many are delving into these caves and digging up creek beds searching for the hidden treasures of Georgia. There have been no big paydays reported, but the fever still remains, burning strong in the hearts of the Gold Belt.

Chapter Fifteen

THE WITCH OF
CEDAR MOUNTAIN

U p a winding mountain pass, not too far from the Dahlonega Gold
Belt, a pile of stones sits in the middle of the road. If you didn't
notice the historical marker, you would chalk it up to another oddity of
the South. Many people say that southerners parade their crazy and never
apologize for the idiosyncrasies people find going down small little roads
in Alabama and Georgia. They even say that these strange landmarks are
treasured and revered by the people who live there, or if they are not,
then they are at least accepted. But this little stone pile doesn't belong to
anyone's crazy Uncle Jessie or Bob or anyone with goats on his roof, but
to Trahlyta and her wish for happiness for all who visit her grave.

Trahlyta, an Indian princess, lived north of Dahlonega on top of
Cedar Mountain. She was told by a witch who lived nearby to walk by a
stream every day and take a drink. "You will grow more beautiful with
each sip," the witch told her. Word spread quickly of her growing beauty.
Hernando De Soto was busy exploring Florida when he heard of her
beauty and swiftly headed north to find the spring, which he believed
could be the fountain of youth.

Trahlyta had a suitor, the Cherokee warrior Wahsega, whom she
rejected. One day, while walking to the spring, Wahsega captured Trahlyta
and took her far away west to his home. She begged and pleaded, but
each day, she grew weaker without her spring and the air from the Blue
Ridge Mountains. As she cried tears of pure gold, she begged him to

Trahlyta's grave, on top of Cedar Mountain.

bury her near her spring so that people could come to lay stones on her grave and what they wished for could be theirs. Honoring her wishes, he brought her home after she died; her body had withered away and lost all its beauty.

Today, her grave is in Stonepile Gap, and the spring, known as Porter Springs, still runs clear and fresh. Porter Springs was once a popular tourist destination. People would go there for spa-type treatments, drinking and bathing in the springs for healing purposes; however, the hotel there burned in the early 1900s, and the area returned back to nature. Now, all that is there is a small farm near the small creek, which runs along the side of the road with no markers or fancy spas. The highway department twice tried to move the grave of Trahlyta, and both times, it had bad fortune and death fell on the crews.

Little is known about the witch of Cedar Mountain. It isn't known if she was an actual witch or a medicine woman. It could be that Trahlyta was the witch, and she made the story up to draw attention away from her magic. Perhaps the focus of this legend shouldn't be on Trahlyta's beauty or her tragic death but on the magic of the springs and how they got such healing powers. It could be possible that this little creek on the side of the road is really the fountain of youth, but I guess we will never know.

Chapter Sixteen

THE PEA RIVER WILD WOMAN

The Pea River is a 154-mile-long river that flows into the Choctawhatchee. "Pea River" comes from the Muscogee name *Talakhatchee*, which means "pea green stream," and it is one of the few rivers in Alabama not called by its original native name. Both the Pea River and the Choctawhatchee are part of the Coastal Plain streams leading out into the Gulf of Mexico in Florida. The Coastal Plain streams are usually considered "black water" due to their color. The black waters are some of the cleanest water in Alabama, not like its sister water basin, the ACF, of which the Chattahoochee River is part, which is potentially the most polluted river basin in the southeastern United States. The Coastal Plain streams and the ACF basin are a stone's throw away from each other, both running through Eufaula and Dothan, Alabama.

Pea River is known for both its swelling waters—often flooding nearby cities such as Elba and Ino, Alabama—and for its fish and wildlife, such as gulf sturgeon and many, many alligators. But Pea River is also famous for a different type of wildlife, one that leaves many victims squealing and screaming in its wake: the Pea River Wild Woman.

The legend says if you drive to the banks below the Pea River Bridge between Opp and Enterprise and call the Wild Woman out while your lights are off, she will surely be standing in front of your car when you turn them back on. When you drive away, she will chase your car all the way across the bridge until you are out of sight—that is, if you are lucky enough to keep your car running. Many people who have tested the Wild Woman myth have had engine trouble or flat tires, preventing their escapes.

Many say Essie is waiting on this old boat ramp, trying to find the right moment to cross the river to be reunited with her son. *Photo courtesy Lori Gwaltney.*

No one really knows where the legend comes from. Some say that the Wild Woman's infant was stolen, and she chases you looking for her baby. Others say she was a weapon-wielding lunatic who wants to kill for sport even after death. But one story seems to be more factually based than others—the story of the missing child.

Ancestors of the first settlers near Pea River tell stories about vicious wildlife all around the river. Mr. Hampton Parish and his worker Mr. Parker, a nearby neighbor, once were attacked by a black bear after trying to save one of Mr. Parish's hogs from the beast. The bear ran Mr. Parker straight up a tree, and Mr. Parker, while still in the tree, hit the bear in the eye with a hunting knife, causing the bear to leave. Allen Carter was attacked by a panther at a place called Jordan Brook's mill soon after. The panther came straight in the door of the mill, and Mr. Carter had to hold it down until some men could come to kill it. Jack Matthews and Jack Sasser were also attacked inside their workplaces or homes by wildcats. But one story of animal attacks could be the most reasonable for the Pea River Wild Woman, and it started when Essie Ligon heard the terrified cries of her child.

Essie Ligon lived near what was called Sylvan Grove, just off the banks of the river. More than likely, she was a slave during this time, but it is undocumented. One day, she had gone to a spring for some water when she heard the cries of her infant. She ran home as fast as she could and found an empty blanket where her child once was. Essie searched for days and days and then weeks and even years, but she never could find her child. It drove her mad, and she became unkempt and unruly. She searched high and low for her child, even grabbing other people's children and claiming them as hers, attacking their mothers aggressively out of anger. She was described as "turned out" after her erratic behavior became too much to bear, and she began to wander the area as a wild woman.

During this time, around 1829, Indians, most likely Creeks, were occupying the area. The settlers had had several run-ins with the local natives, losing oxen and getting into heated gunfights with them. Some African slave women were down by the banks of the river one day, washing clothes, when Essie walked up. They saw an African child, clothed in native clothes, playing alone on the other side of the river. As the women chatted about what he would be doing alone and why he was in native clothing, he looked up at Essie. Essie looked in his eyes and knew she had found her son.

It was after a rain, and the river had swelled; the water was moving rapidly. Essie couldn't swim, but in her excitement, she jumped into Pea River, trying to get to her child. The women tried to stop her, but she got in too fast. She turned to them with elation saying, "See! I knew he was here. A 'coon must have taken him to an Indian woman!" (Raccoons often tried to drag off small babies.) Though she tried to swim, the swift water began to drag her downriver, and she drowned. The women reported her drowning, but they couldn't find her body (not that anyone tried very hard to find her). Some field workers found her body downstream, washed up on shore, a few weeks later. Beasts and birds had scavenged her body. Since she was "turned out" with no one to claim her, the rest of her remains were buried in a shallow grave by the edge of the water.

Many believe that Essie is still waiting on the banks of the Pea River, trying to find the right moment to cross to be reunited with her son. Either way, she seems to be very aggressive and wild, turning on people who she thinks might have her son. So beware if you have car trouble by the bridge between Opp and Enterprise: you might just be chased by the Pea River Wild Woman.

Chapter Seventeen

THE GHOSTS OF BROOKSIDE DRIVE

Not far from Pea River is a home in Opp, Alabama, nestled on top of a hill and surrounded by the beauty of nature. In springtime, the wisteria winds its way through the thirty azalea bushes, and the bees buzz around the ever-changing colors of the hydrangeas. The cardinals and jays chirp, and the squirrels use the carport as an opener for their hickory nuts. No one would look at this 1950s home and think it anything but tranquil and desirable to passersby, but within its walls, a nightmare lies.

The tale began in the fall of 1988, when a new doctor came to town in search of a home for his large family of seven. Seeing the home and needing the 3,100 square feet, the doctor and his wife decided to ask if the homeowner would be willing to sell. To their good fortune, the lovely widow who lived there agreed, and by January, their rowdy bunch moved in. As they were pulling in for the first time, their son made the remark that the house looked a little too much like the one on Elm Street (in the movie *Nightmare on Elm Street*), but the doctor's wife was willing to give it some much-needed love and care, and slowly over the next ten years, she made their house a beautiful home.

One thing was certain about the home: it had its own personality, almost its own marrow, as if it breathed its own life, fueled by the wild and ardent energy of the five children and the zoolike atmosphere of dogs, cats, birds, reptiles and rodents that were their pets. The house was in a constant mode of chaos. The older girls were always fighting over clothes, the son was always stomping down the stairs like an elephant and the youngest was

The house on Brookside Drive. No one would believe the nightmares hidden within its walls.

constantly roller-skating or playing golf on the hardwood floors in her room. Dinners were a sight to see: food fights and thrown rolls, loud laughter and the clinking of what seemed like a million plates and glasses. Life was good for this wild bunch, despite the ever-present ghosts that they just seemed to accept as part of the family.

They first noticed the man they called "Mr. Allred" within the first year of living at their new home. Lori, who was about thirteen at the time, woke up to a man standing over her bed. He was tall, thin and older, and his black suit jacket was too short for his arms. He had on a large round hat that almost looked too big for his head. Lori screamed, and Stevie, fourteen years old then, came running into the room. As soon as he turned on the lights, the man was gone. Slowly, they all began to see the man here and there and assumed he was the husband of the former owner Mrs. Allred, so they began calling him Mr. Allred. Mr. Allred's ghost was a protector, a watcher and a soft soul; he just seemed to belong to the house.

Later, the youngest daughter, Michelle, then about age ten, looked out her bedroom window and saw a little girl in a pink dress jumping rope in the front yard. Michelle went outside to find the girl, but there was no girl to be found. She searched all around the property, and when she heard someone whisper, "Brittney," in her ear but found no one next to her, she ran inside and up the stairs and didn't tell a soul. Michelle says it's possible Brittney played in her room, too, because her dad would come upstairs often to tell her to stop jump roping, and she wouldn't even be in her room.

There were also phantom voices. Each family member tells a story of separate occasions on which another member of the family would call his or her name. Two times the name was called, and two times the family member in question would call out answering. The third time the name was called, the voice became deep and angry, and the word almost ended in a growl. The story usually resulted in the family member leaving the house because he or she would realize there was no one else home. Stevie even left in nothing but a towel once, going to a friend's house until his parents came home.

It seemed as if the appearance of these voices brought something else along with it, and as the years went by, the spirits got darker. By the time Michelle was about fourteen, her older sisters, Christy and Kathy, were grown and out of the house, but the remaining family members were being forcefully oppressed by the energy of the house. Their friends became nervous to even visit, and the kids didn't want to sleep alone. Whatever was going on seemed to be worse in the upstairs bedrooms, where Lori and Michelle slept. They both encountered terrifying sightings, such as floating blobs of what looked like chocolate pudding or orange-colored bushes. Lori complained almost daily about black roses and chandeliers floating across the room.

It began to take a toll on their sleep and health. Lori was having night terrors and dropping grades, and Michelle's forced insomnia caused her to contract mononucleosis, which seemed to zap her immune system and caused her weight to drop to a sickly level.

Both the girls had paranoid feelings of being watched in their bedrooms. Lori nailed quilts all around the bunk bed she slept in so that she had some sort of protection, and Michelle stayed up nights on end because of the demonic dreams she would have, praying and reciting the Lord's Prayer until she could no longer stay awake. Both tell stories about feeling as if something entered their arms up to their shoulders before backing out again, and Michelle remembers having red marks on her arms like someone had grabbed her very hard. One night, Michelle even felt something get in her bed with her and turned over to see a man with gray skin and no eyes lying next to her. She ran down the stairs to get in bed with her parents, but there was no room because both Stevie and Lori were already there.

Their animals seemed to be targets of attacks as well. Light bulbs would explode near them, spraying glass all around, and doors would slam on the animals without provocation. The cats were often slung from the porch swing, and the dogs were constantly growling at the air, especially in the girls' rooms. Strange noises began to emanate from upstairs, and the kids' father was always checking to see if someone had broken in. The family dealt with the strange occurrences as best they could. Eventually, the doctor got a job in another city, and the family moved out.

If you ask them, however, whether the activity had lasting effects on them, they playfully agree that they could stand a dose of therapy because of it. It took a toll on their health and well-being during and after, causing years of insomnia for Michelle and night terrors for Lori. There isn't a whole lot of history on the property. The home was built in the 1950s and was owned by Dr. Burgess and then by the Allreds. The truth is that no one can say why the house had so much activity. The kids do think their careless play with a Ouija board while they were teenagers could have opened up the opportunity for this oppressive activity, especially since the house already had paranormal activity with Mr. Allred and Brittney; but since moving, none of the family claims any amount of activity compared to what happened at Brookside Drive.

The new owners claim no paranormal activity at all; however, Michelle disagrees. During a return visit a few years ago, she was pushed down the driveway by an unseen force, which was enough of a warning for her to stay away for good, and she suggests you do the same.

Chapter Eighteen

HUGGIN' MOLLY

Twelve miles from the rolling waters of the Chattahoochee is a small creek running through the center of Henry County, Alabama. It was named Yatta Abba, translated as "a grove of dogwood trees," by the Muskogee Nation Indians who lived along its banks. In 1822, the city of Abbeville was named after the creek, now called Abbie Creek. While more famous for the 121 men of Company G of the Fifteenth Alabama Regiment, led by none other than William C. Oates, and their immortalized battle at Gettysburg's Little Round Top during the Civil War, it seems Abbeville is notorious for something a little darker. Huggin' Molly is the character of nightmares for little children all around the city.

Huggin' Molly stories have been around since the early 1900s. She is often described as very tall, almost close to seven feet, and she was as big around as a bale of cotton. One version says that Molly lost her arm as a child, and she was given a golden arm in its place. Several boys in town knew that one day Molly would die, and they could steal her golden arm. Upon her death, they dug Molly up and took her arm. As they began to fill in her grave, a voice came up saying, "I want my golden arm!" The boys began to run, and the voice continued after them, "Come back! Come back!" One of the boys was caught by the hooded figure behind him. He was squeezed so tight he could not breathe, and the figure screamed so loud he thought he would die from the shock. The other boys fought to free him, and they ran for dear life all the way home. They melted down Molly's arm and sold it off, piece by piece. Molly still roams the grounds of Abbeville looking for her golden arm, not knowing the boys and her arm are long gone.

There is story after story from Abbeville citizens about meeting her on the street. Many say if she saw you, she'd chase you down, give you a huge hug and scream in your ear. Each story seems to have the hooded figure walking behind a person after dark. Such fear was struck in the citizens of Abbeville that it was rare for anyone to venture out after dark.

One woman stood on her front porch as her son walked home. She saw a hooded figure walking behind him. Each step of his the figure matched; as he began to pick up the pace, so did the figure. Eventually, the mother screamed out to her son to run. He ran, and they both jumped inside, locking the door behind them and leaving the figure on the front porch. Another story was of a man who was delivering groceries. He heard steps behind him in the same manner until he ran home and locked the door.

It seems that Huggin' Molly was so terrifying that rumors of her spread to other towns. In 1908, the editor of the *Headland Post* gave a warning to the "Woman in Black" that she would be shot on sight. Nobody knows if there was a copycat Molly actually going around scaring people or if it was really Molly herself, searching for her arm in nearby towns.

Huggin' Molly is more than just a bedtime story for many who live in Abbeville.

Stories of the woman in black and Huggin' Molly have held their places in Abbeville's history. There is even a restaurant named directly after Molly. It sells "sandwitches" and the Molly burger and even has "comeback" sauce.

It seems Huggin' Molly will always be a part of Abbeville's history. Whether a way to keep kids out of trouble and home after dark or a real live folk tale, many will never know; if you ask citizens of Abbeville, they will say with as many eyewitness stories as they've been told in their lifetime, there is no way she is just a legend.

Part IV

NATIVE AMERICAN LEGENDS

Chapter Nineteen

BLOOD MOUNTAIN AND THE IMMORTALS

Blood Mountain is a peak on the Appalachian Trail just inside the Chattahoochee National Forest. Its summit reaches 4,458 feet high, one of the highest in Georgia. How Blood Mountain got its name is a dispute. Some claim it to be from the lichen that grows on the Catawba trees in the wilderness, but others blame the bloody battle between the Creeks and Cherokees at Slaughter Gap, the winner of which Blood Mountain would go to as a prize. The Creeks ceded to the Cherokees, who consider Blood Mountain holy land because of the immortals, or Nunnehi, who live there.

Nunnehi were known to the Cherokees as the "Spirit people who live anywhere." Nunnehi are said to be invisible unless they want to be seen, and then, they just look like everybody else. The Nunnehi are believed to inhabit Blood Mountain and help wanderers or people who are lost find their way home, and they were also known to have helped the Cherokees in battle against the Creeks to protect their homeland.

The Over-hill Indian Nation tells a story about a ten- or twelve-year-old child who was playing near the river and became tired. While he was building up a wall of stones to catch fish, a man said, "Well, that's pretty hard work. Come with me, and I will give you rest and a good meal." The boy went with the man to a cabin, and his wife was there. They fed him and let him rest. A man from town, Udsi'skalä, came in and spoke with the boy. The boy felt pretty safe in the cabin. Udsi'skalä told the boy to follow the river down, and he would find his way home.

The tree at Mountain Crossings at Walasi-yi holds the "soles" of many who were lost and then found on Blood Mountain.

While walking, his mother came running to him, shouting out and saying, "He is here! He is not killed or lost on Blood Mountain!" The boy said, "I was not lost. I went to a cabin where a woman and man fed me and let me rest, and I left with Udsi'skalä." Udsi'skalä was with the people, and he said to the boy, "I have not seen you, and you've been gone since yesterday, noon." His mother shouted for joy and yelled out, "Many times thank you!" She said it had to have been the Nunnehi people who helped her son.

Also, just north of Blood Mountain was a small hollowed-out spot in the ground believed to be a chimney of the Nunnehi's underworld home, and hunters and fishers would often go there to get warm before heading home, especially if they had stayed too late and couldn't get off the mountain until daylight.

But another theory about the Nunnehi leads us to Bigfoot. Many stories from Blood Mountain point to the Nunnehi being none other than the hairy man. Reports of drumming have often been heard on the mountain, and a round area, sunken in and piled with soft leaves and pine straw as bedding, has been found. Many would throw logs or trash in the hole to fill it in. When they came back later, the logs and trash were thrown far from the hole. Some claim it to be the entrance to the Nunnehi Township, and others claim it to be the bedding of a Bigfoot. The Bigfoot Field Research Organization has investigated several sightings in the area and believes the drumming could be mistaken for wood knocks of a Sasquatch, and the group also reports many other signs that Sasquatch live in the area.

Blood Mountain is not a place for the fainthearted or the novice hiker. Many hikers have been lost on the mountain, cold, tired and hungry; yet very few have stayed lost for long. Each lost hiker claims he was rescued by someone who led him the right way or that he was led by fear from noises in the woods. One man who was visiting claims he rescued a woman who was suffering from hypothermia. "She would have died sitting right next to a fire. It just wasn't warm enough for her little wet bones. I wrapped her up and dropped her off at the hostel." He chuckled, "I never even told her my name!" There is always a miraculous story about how these lost people found their way back to the tree filled with hiking boots at the Mountain Crossings at Walasi-yi outpost at Neel's Gap on the top of the mountain.

No matter whether it is the hairy man or the Nunnehi, the mountain seems to be guarded by a protector, someone who has been there as far back as America's history has been told, and someone who seems to be immortal.

Chapter Twenty

THE MOUNDS AND THE OLD SACRED THINGS

Some of the most interesting and mysterious pieces of history you can find in the United States are Indian mounds. Mounds were used for ceremonies, burial and status by many native tribes. Many Indian nations say that mounds were first built by another people, possibly immortal spirits or maybe even the sky people. However they were first built, there was a sacred and methodical way that the mounds and homes, often referred to as "townhouses," were built among the tribes of the Chattahoochee.

Mounds were often built on level bottomlands by rivers to have smooth ground for ceremony and ball play. A circle of stone or built-up earth would be formed and a fire made in the center of the circle. It was usually put near the body of a lately passed holy man or chief. There would be a council of men from different clans who would bless or curse objects such as eagle feathers, horns and seven colors of beads. They would curse them so as to curse any intruders that might steal them.

The mounds were built up with earth, and it was piled high above the stones. Some mounds are so big it is questionable how many it took to build them and how the builders did it with so few tools. One of the largest mounds is as high as sixty-two feet up. Each mound was usually given its own purpose, which could be council area, burial site, cremation or even trash disposal.

While building the mounds used for townhouses and ceremonies, Indians would let down a hollow cedar trunk to protect the fire and build up the earth around the fire, smoothing off the top of it. Then, the townhouses would be built on top of this smoothed surface. Many mounds would be capped off with levels of wet clay that would be heated by the sun, harden like rock and protect the things within the mounds from intruders.

The fire within the mound was one of the most sacred things. There was usually a mound specifically for fire. It was called the "everlasting fire" because it was never left unattended and was never allowed to go out. The fire keeper would stay with the fire all year, keeping it smoldering. Everyone in the settlement would start fires from the sacred or everlasting fire. Once a year, the people in the tribe would put out their fires and return to the fire keeper for new fire. This was usually done during the Green Corn Dance or Festival, because it was a time of renewal and rebirth in the community.

Fire was not the only sacred thing. Often sacred items were kept in a central location with protectors or holy men who watched over them. They often included turtle-shell drums or rattles, eagle feathers and medicine. Cherokee legend speaks of such a box that was taken by a rival tribe. Losing the sacred

A bust of a chief or a sacred member of the Swift Creek tribe.

items was a great time of trouble for the Cherokees. When all the old things were stolen, the Cherokees became a different and more modern race.

The significance of the mounds is of even more importance today. Archaeologically, each mound is like a time capsule, laying out the history and tradition of these settlements. Pottery and small items referred to as "sherds" are carefully sifted out, one shovel full at a time. Each small item has its own story to tell; it tells how old it is, where it came from and who made it, as well as its significance. Perhaps one day, one of the sacred boxes will be discovered to reveal lost traditions and the native people can regain a part of their culture.

What is so remarkable is that some of these mounds have been around dating back to the BC era, and they will probably still be here for several more centuries or until the earth is no more. With ever-growing technology, each aspect of these mounds brings us closer to the traditions and rituals of these great societies. Each one tells us a tale of just how similar cultures were along the Chattahoochee, but they also reveal all the subtle differences that make each one unique.

Chapter Twenty-one

THE KOLOMOKI MOUNDS

K olomoki, formerly known as the Mercier Mounds, is one of the rarest and most impressive archaeological sites in the southeastern United States. It is located in the lower Chattahoochee Valley of Southwest Georgia, immediately south and west of Little Kolomoki Creek. Kolomoki Creek flows into the Chattahoochee River seven miles northwest of the mound site.

Although surrounded by several other mound sites, such as Mandeville, Ocmulgee River, Chattahoochee Valley, Marksville, Baytown and Mounds plantation, Kolomoki is rare in the fact that it is so large in population and also that it is so far away from the Chattahoochee River, which many believe would have offered even more resources to the settlement. Consensus is that Kolomoki was positioned to take advantage of more productive agricultural lands and nut-bearing trees; but it is also believed to have served as a nexus of settlements for ceremony and trade.

Kolomoki was believed to have been established by Swift Creek Woodland cultures and the Early Weeden Island culture later derived from the Swift Creek with less than 1 percent of pottery samples from the Early Mississippian period. Kolomoki became one of the main archaeological sites in the southeastern United States, starting in the 1930s by William McKinley and Edward Palmer, both associated with the Smithsonian Institute. Intensive work began in 1948 by William Sears, but most impressively, digs are still going on today with much more to learn.

The Kolomoki settlement began with the abandonment of Mandeville settlement in AD 350 and ran through AD 750. The settlement was divided into four phases: I, II, III and IV. Phases I and II maintained the same population level; however, in AD 550 and the beginning of the Late Woodland period, population declined by one-half when the ritual and ceremony of living in tightknit groups became less formal and scattered. Because of more household autonomy, Kolomoki IV saw the decline in settlements, and the sight was abandoned by AD 750.

Kolomoki has nine mounds. Historical accounts offer the existence of several other mounds and a large earthen wall or enclosure. The largest mound has a height of fifty-seven feet. It is shaped very much like a flat pyramid, and it is as large as a football field on top, making it the largest land-based mound in Georgia. As stated, each mound held its own purpose. Some were for ceremonies, some for burial and one seemed to have the sole purpose of holding large wooden poles. It is unknown if the poles were used in a game, much like baseball or lacrosse, or if they were used during ceremonies and meetings to notify if the settlement was a peaceful one or one at war. During the examination of the poles, red clay with white clay underneath was found. White clay would have signified a peace town. It

There are eighty-one steps to the top of the largest mound at Kolomoki.

is possible that the settlement later became a war town, changing the pole colors to red.

One of the more interesting finds is the amount of energy used in the mortuary rituals. White clay was often used as a symbol of sky and purity. Over the white clay is a layer of red clay symbolizing earth and the return of the body to earth. Often, the women were in charge of the mortuary rituals. Not everyone was buried; there are signs of one mound being used for cremation. Many believe those who were buried held some stature within the settlement.

There is also a mysterious alignment of the mounds to the stars, and the symbolism on their pottery offers a clue into a very ritualistic motif of renewal, rebirth and fertility much like the Aztec civilization's beliefs. No doubt many festivals and ceremonies were held, such as the renewal of fire and the Green Corn Festival. This all seemed to decline during Kolomoki phase III, when autonomy began within households. Thomas J. Pluckhahn, archaeologist, argued that Middle Woodland ceremonialism collapsed under the weight of its own success.

An interesting and conspiracy-driven note has to do with what William Sears might have found at the site in the late 1940s and '50s that the Kolomoki museum didn't want released. Perhaps it was the evidence of human sacrifice. The disappearance of all his notes and maps remains a mystery today. Sears wrote a letter to a colleague in 1993 blaming the museum staff for the disappearance of his hard work. Exhaustive searches have been completed to no avail. It is also an important note that not all the mounds have been excavated. One had a cap of white clay that was so hard that archaeologists joked that only an earthquake and dynamite could remove it.

Kolomoki is legendary in its size and historical importance, being one of the largest settlements north of the Aztec civilization in Mexico. It is the largest site in Georgia, second only to the Macon Plateau. Kolomoki is, today, one of Georgia's most treasured state parks. The park offers tours of the mounds as well as a museum, hiking, fishing and camping.

Chapter Twenty-two

NACOOCHEE MOUNDS

Another significant mound site in Georgia is known as the Nacoochee Indian Mounds, or the Sautee Nacoochee Indian Mounds. Nacoochee holds its own legendary status in the heart of every Georgian and tourist who goes through the small alpine community of Helen, Georgia. Despite its touristy twist of wineries and antique shops, the Nacoochee area just outside of Helen holds an interesting piece of American history.

The Chattahoochee River flows from the Blue Ridge Mountains at Unicoi Gap, rolls down passing north of the Nacoochee Mound and the feet of the Yonah Mountain and drops into a geological rift that flows to Columbus, Georgia. If you visit the mound today, you will see a beautiful gazebo on top of it and the droves of cattle that surround it, grazing on grass all around. You can read the historical marker of the Indian version of *Romeo and Juliet*. The story is of the beautiful Cherokee princess Nacoochee, who fell in love with a Chickasaw brave, Sautee. Nacoochee's father was Chief Wahoo. Wahoo allowed the Chickasaws to pass through the valley so long as they kept to the Indian trail and camped only where he told them to. Nacoochee was curious, so she spied on the Chickasaws as they set up camp. She saw Sautee, and she was attracted to him. They met and spent several days together in a cave known only to Nacoochee. When Chief Wahoo found out, he was angry and captured Sautee. It started a war between the two tribes because Sautee was the son of the Chickasaw chief. Wahoo chose a day to throw Sautee from the top of the mountains. Just at the last moment, Nacoochee ran to Sautee, and

This Nacoochee mound is often called the "Romeo and Juliet" of Indian mounds.

they fell together from the cliffs of Yonah Mountain (translated as Bear Mountain). Because of their sorrow, the Chickasaw and the Cherokee chiefs lived peacefully ever after. This is a popular Georgia myth, but the reality is much more confusing than the legend.

Some say the legend is false because Chickasaw tribes lived three hundred miles east of the Nacoochee territory. Some also say that archaeologists didn't even discover Cherokee artifacts at the mound, only Creek. The truth is that Chickasaws did live in what is now Habersham and White Counties up until the American Revolution, and directly south of them were Catawba Indian villages, though many people believed the Catawbas only resided in South Carolina until the Trail of Tears. All of this is contrary to what the mainstream believes as far as territories.

The original name for the Nacoochee village was Nokose. *Nokose* is actually a Creek term for bear. When the Cherokees settled in the area, they pronounced nokose as "n'goochee." Early European settlers then began to pronounce it "nacoochee." The word *sautee* is also a Creek word; originally, it was pronounced "sawate," which means "the Racoon People." The Muskogee Creeks actually called the area Sawakee, which later became called Sautee by the locals.

Prior to AD 500, the Nacoochee Valley was occupied by Swift Creek Indians; this was proven by the archaeological dig at the Nacoochee mounds in 1915 by the Heye Foundation. It located seventy-five human burials, some of them from a later time period. This was unknown to the first European settlers, who believed the Creeks were actually Cherokees.

There was belief that the area was the site of the city of Guaxule, a city Hernando De Soto mentioned during his exploration of Georgia while searching for the "city of gold"; however, there are four other locations believed to be Guaxule, and none of them has been verified. It has also been argued by expeditions of General George Chicken that the place was the site of two Cherokee villages in the 1710s.

What was so strange about the Swift Creek Nacoochee settlement is that it literally seemed to die out within weeks. It is believed that the monarch butterfly carried pathogens from Mexico to the Southern Highlands, causing a hemorrhagic plague, much like the Mexican Highlands plague that wiped out the Aztecs. The plague would have been much like cholera, causing a quick evacuation of all bodily fluids and an anticoagulation of the blood supply. It would give the infected less than twenty-four hours to live. This plague, coupled with the introduction of the bow and arrow, making wartime more deadly, wiped out almost 95 percent of the population. It is considered one of the first holocausts in America's known history.

Nacoochee's legendary status as a lovers' leap has been told all over the Southeast. Other similar legends of star-crossed lovers are Noccalulla Falls in Gadsden, Alabama, Lovers Leap over the Chattahoochee River in Columbus, Georgia, and Chewacla State Park in Auburn, Alabama. It is unknown if this was a common issue among Indian civilizations or if there was one story that originated the legend that just grew into each culture.

Perhaps Nacoochee isn't well known for its historical accuracy, but it is known as one of Georgia's most beloved legends, and the cute little mound in the center of a cow field will always be a conversational tale along the Chattahoochee River.

Chapter Twenty-three

THE RABBIT TRICKSTER

In Indian mythology, there is generally no difference between man and animal. In the beginning of all mythology, you can find all creatures alike, living and working together, be they men or beasts. But when man, by his aggressive nature and selfish disregard of others, provokes animals against him, their lives are ever separated.

One of the greatest legends of Indian culture is that of the Rabbit Trickster. The rabbit carries over through several different tribes from Creek, Catawba, Cherokee and many more. Rabbit is often malicious and is often beaten at his own game, but not always. He is often very clever and crafty.

One famous trickster tale is "Why the Possum's Tail Is Bare." You will find variations of it in many different cultures; one of the most prominent along the Chattahoochee is the Cherokee version. The Cherokee version states that the possum used to have a long and bushy tail, and he was so proud of it he would comb it every morning. He would even sing about it at the dance. The rabbit had lost his tail when the bear pulled it out, and so he was very jealous of the possum.

There was to be a great council, and rabbit was in charge of inviting everyone. He passed the possum and asked if he intended to be there. The possum said he would come if he could have a special seat because his tail was so special that he believed he ought to sit where everyone could see his tail. Rabbit agreed to the seat and even told possum he would have someone sit beside him and brush his tail.

LEGENDS, LORE & TRUE TALES OF THE CHATTAHOOCHEE

Rabbit went to cricket, who was the best cutter in town. He told cricket just what to do to possum's tail. Cricket went to possum's house, and possum allowed cricket to fix his tail for the night. Possum drifted to sleep never knowing cricket wrapped his hair in a red ribbon, all the while cutting his hair to the root.

When it came time for possum to dance and sing, he unwrapped his tail and twirled in a big circle, and everyone shouted. "See how beautiful my tail is?" possum said. They shouted some more. "See how it floats across the floor?" They shouted even louder. Possum was confused about why they were laughing so loudly, so he looked down at his tail and saw it cut all the way to the skin so that his tail looked like a lizard's. He was so shocked and ashamed that he rolled over helplessly on the ground and grinned, as the possum does to this day when taken by surprise.

Creek mythology tells a story of how "Rabbit Steals Fire." All the people came together and asked, "How do we obtain fire?" The chief said, "Rabbit will get us fire," and so they sent rabbit to obtain fire. He went across the great water to the East. He was gladly received, and a dance was arranged. Rabbit wore a headpiece with four pieces of rosin on his head. He danced about the sacred fire of the people from the East. He danced closer and closer to the flames. As the people from the East began to bow to the fire, rabbit bowed down as well, and the rosin caught fire. The people of the East were angry, and they chased rabbit to the water's edge, where he jumped in with his head aflame. He swam back across the great water, thus obtaining fire from the East.

The best Cherokee myth of the rabbit getting a taste of his own medicine is that of "Why the Deer's Teeth Are Blunt and What Became of the Rabbit." Rabbit was angry because the deer had won horns during a race that the rabbit cheated in. Rabbit gnawed a grapevine almost in two, went back a piece and jumped the vine. He kept running and jumping until deer wanted to try it. When deer tried, the vine held him, threw him over his head and left him bruised and bleeding. Rabbit said, "Deer, let me see your teeth." So deer showed him his teeth, which were like the wolf's. "No wonder you can't gnaw the vine; your teeth are too blunt to bite anything. Let me sharpen them for you like mine." Rabbit got a hard stone and filed and filed the deer's teeth until they were worn down almost to the gums. "It hurts," said the deer, but the rabbit convinced him he was fine. The deer tried again but could not bite at all. "Now this time you have paid for your horns," said the rabbit, and he jumped away. Ever since then, deer's teeth have been so blunt that he can only chew grass and leaves.

"He danced about the sacred fire of the people from the East." *Art courtesy of Brandon Stoker.*

Now deer was very angry at rabbit for filing his teeth but kept still and pretended to be his friend until rabbit was off his guard. One day, they were going along together, and deer challenged rabbit to jump against him. The rabbit was a great jumper, and so he agreed at once. Deer said, "Let's see if you can jump this branch. We will go back a piece and when I say, 'Ku,' then we will both run and jump."

So they went back a piece, and when the deer gave the word *ku*, they ran for the stream. Rabbit landed on the other side when he jumped. But the deer had stopped on the bank, and when rabbit looked back, deer had conjured the stream so that it was a large river. Rabbit was never able to get back again and is still on the other side. The rabbit that we know now is only the little thing that came afterward.

Chapter Twenty-four

THE ORIGIN OF EARTH

I t seems that every culture has a creation myth, and Native Americans are no different. Considered by many "cosmogonist myths," these stories often include animals and geological and astronomical symbolism.

It is often hard to decipher how much of modern-day Christianity has been added to these stories. Many tales include an ark and a flooded earth. Missionaries were often sent to visit villages, and many Indian cultures incorporated undertones of the Trinity or biblical stories into their tales. Even as close as 1975, there were government-sponsored Native American boarding schools. It somehow became the "duty" of America to "purge" the Indians of their savage gods and beliefs. They took thousands of children from their mothers' arms and put them in religious educational institutions. It was a trying time. Insolent children who did not conform to their new identities were beaten, and many died from abuse or starvation. Despite these cultural setbacks, many of the origin tales still remain. The two most popular tales along the Chattahoochee are from the Creeks and the Cherokees.

The Yuchi Creek origin of Earth states in the beginning that water covered everything. It was asked, "Who will make land?" Lockchew, the crawfish, said, "I will make land appear." So he went down to the bottom and began to stir up mud with his tail and hands, and he rolled it into a ball.

The owners of the land at the bottom of the water said, "Who is disturbing our land?" They got near Lockchew, but he would stir up the mud so they could not see him. He worked until there was land piled up above the water.

The buzzard flapped his wings when he was tired and made hills and valleys.

The land was soft. Someone asked, "Who will spread out the land so that it will dry and become hard?" Some said Ah-yok the hawk could do it, and others said Yah-tee the buzzard could do it. Yah-tee began to spread out the dirt, but when his wings got tired, he flapped them; thus, he created hills and valleys where the land was still soft.

It was very dark, so someone asked, "Who will make the light?" Yohah, the star, said, "I will make the light." It was then asked, "Who will make more light?" Shar-pah, the moon, said, "I will make more light." Shar-pah made more light, but it was still dark. T-cho, the sun, said, "You are my children; I am your mother. I will make the light; I will shine for you." She went to the East and began to shine; as she passed, a drop of her blood fell from her onto the ground and made the first people, the Yuchi.

The Cherokees believe Earth is a great island floating in a sea of water and suspended at each of the four points by a cord hanging down from the sky that is of solid rock. When the world grows old, the people will die, the cords will break and the earth will sink down into the ocean.

When all was water at first, the animals were above in Gâlun'lâti, the arch (or ark), but it was very crowded. The little water beetle offered to go see if there was land. He could find none but brought up some soft mud, which grew and spread until it became an island. It was afterward fastened to the sky, but no one remembers who did this.

The Cherokee legend was more than likely influenced more by Christian America. The legend goes on to speak of another who created more of the world in seven days, and those who stayed awake during those seven days were granted the ability to see at night, such as the owl and panther. It also speaks of a world under this one, which has the Christian undertone of hell or the suggestion of a supernatural veil.

It is unlikely that many of the Creeks were influenced as much by Christianity because they were less likely to conform to the white man ways and often warred with those who tried to interfere with their culture. However, no matter the culture, there is an underlying need inside all of us to know where we came from and how we got started. Somehow, we all have the need to know the origin of Earth.

Chapter Twenty-five

THE ORIGIN OF CORN

Much like the origin of Earth, we have a desire to know where our food source comes from. Corn is a food staple all over the world. Wheat or barley is often referred to as corn in many cultures. Even in biblical times, wheat was called corn. Western culture began its love affair with corn with Christopher Columbus when he discovered it in Cuba. Early European settlers called American corn "Indian Corn" because of the important role it played in Native American culture. Being a staple food source for the Indian, corn is celebrated in ceremonies, status and even in its origin.

Several tribes who lived along the Chattahoochee celebrated what is called the Green Corn Festival. The Green Corn Festival is a ceremonial dance and celebration of the first ripe and ready-to-eat corn of the season along with spiritual renewal and forgiveness for wrongs against the community. It is performed by the Yuchis, Seminoles, Creeks, Cherokees and Catawbas, as well as the Catawbas' mother tribe, the Iroquois.

Along with this celebration is the story of the origin of corn. Each tribe has a few different versions of the origin. Most have a nurturing aspect, a "birth" of corn from a motherly source. They also tend to have the orphan, thrown-away or wild boy aspect. The Yuchi Creeks actually have three different versions they tell, the following being the most prominent among the Chattahoochee tribes.

One day, an old woman was walking along the river when she saw a drop of blood in the water. She gathered up the blood and sand from the water. She took it home and put it in a jar. She kept it there under a blanket for ten months, until she discovered a boy had grown in its place. She nurtured the boy, and when he was older, she gave him a bow and arrow and taught him to hunt birds. Once he had mastered that, she taught him to hunt squirrel, then deer and finally bear.

One day, when he returned from hunting, she made him blue corn dumplings and beans. He ate and wondered where she had gotten such delightful food. He asked her, but she refused to tell him. The next day, he told the old woman he was going hunting, but instead, he spied on her. He watched her enter a room. She lifted her skirt and began to rub her thighs and feet. Corn fell into the bucket from them. He returned home and refused to eat her dumplings. She said, "Why do you not eat?" He said, "I have seen you produce corn from your body." She said, "You must not tell others where the corn comes from."

She then warned him not to go over the mountain. He went there anyway and beheld a lovely valley below. When he returned home, he appeared lonely.

The old woman said, "You have been beyond the mountain. I will make you a lovely garment and let you go. Bring me a singing bird from the woods." So she made him a headdress, a garment and a flute. She taught him to play the flute, and the singing bird landed in his headdress and sang the melody he played on the flute.

She said, "You will go to the valley and come to a home where three women live. The one who cooks for you will be your wife. Marry her and bring her home for me to meet." The young boy went to the valley and met the women, and one of them offered to cook for him. He married the girl, and they tarried there for some time with her people. He saw the people suffering for food to eat. He told them, "Follow me to the river." He threw some logs in the river and played his flute. When the bird sang on his headdress, the fish came up, and the people shot them with bows and arrows.

Chufee (rabbit) saw the man and became jealous he had a wife. Chufee stole the headdress and flute and ran away. He tried to make music, thinking he could gain a wife, but the flute made no music. He became so angry that he struck the singing bird, injuring its feathers. The people pursued Chufee and captured him. They gave the headdress and the flute back to the young man.

The young man decided it was time for his wife to meet the old woman, and they returned to his mother's home. When they reached the home, it was all different. Where his home once stood were some green stalks, and the old woman was gone. When he returned again to where his mother's home had been, the stalks were dried, and the grain was hard. He built a rock house, gathered the grains and put them in the house.

Corn is still a dominating crop along the Chattahoochee Trace.

He returned again and saw all the birds gathered around the house trying to knock it down. The owl tried to knock it down, flying into the house until it became hump-shouldered. The eagle tried but flew over the house instead. They could not knock it down.

The hawk flew into the house until it drove its neck in, making it have a short neck ever since. It knocked down the house. The birds flew in and gathered the grains. Some crows were in the air fighting over the grain, and some grains fell. The young man took them and carried them to his new home. He planted the grains and from them sprang corn. And that is how corn came to be.

Part V

TRUE STORIES NOT TO BE FORGOTTEN

Chapter Twenty-six

THE WALL AT
FORT MOUNTAIN

Fort Mountain is a strange and enigmatic place, to say the least. Fort Mountain State Park guards the foothills of the Appalachians at the southern end of the Blue Ridge Mountains near Ellijay, Georgia. Although built mostly on land donated by a former Atlanta mayor, there is one piece of the park that was there long before it became a state park. Its puzzling and cryptic beginning leaves natives and non-natives alike scratching their heads. Rocks that aren't native to the area, many of them rather large in size, are piled together in varying heights for 855 feet along the ground. What time period it was built in is even in question, some saying AD 500 and some saying AD 1500. Many believe when the wall was built, it was much, much taller. The question to ask is, "Who built it?"

One belief is that the Welsh prince Madoc, or Madog ab Owain Gwynedd, built the wall. Prince Madoc was a brilliant naval commander during the reign of his father, Owain Gwynedd. After his father's death in AD 1169, Madoc and a group of Welshman made a series of expeditions to the Americas, landing in what is currently Fort Morgan, Alabama, just outside Mobile. Had it not been for Chief Oconostota of the Cherokees, Prince Madoc might have well gone missing from history, for as we all know, history books say Christopher Columbus discovered America in 1492 and was the first to explore it.

The old Chief Oconostota told John Sevier, the first governor of Tennessee, that many of the forts used by the natives were built by the first white people to visit the Americas. It was believed that Prince Madoc and his men made a series of trips using waterways, such as the Alabama and Chattahoochee Rivers, moving all the way up into Ohio. The natives said they were "yellow-haired giants." They were eventually all but destroyed by the native people.

It is not certain that Prince Madoc is the one who built the wall at Fort Mountain, but many other locations in North America have unearthed Welsh helmets and breast plates and skeletons that were Caucasoid—one that was even nine feet, eight inches tall in Jennings County, Indiana. These artifacts at least give Prince Madoc his own legend and place in American history.

Cherokee natives also speak of a race of people they refer to as "moon-eyed people" who could have built the wall. There is some indication that the yellow-haired giants were the same as the moon-eyed people; however, there are several other interpretations of the moon-eyed people. Most interpret them to be white people, but not in the sense often used to describe European settlers. These white people were a pale-skinned race with very large blue eyes that were sensitive to the light, and they normally only came out at night. On a full moon night, they were completely blind, hence "moon eyed."

Caucasoid races, or "white races," are actually discovered through many different cultures where they would not be expected. Even China had the

Fort Mountain Lake over Chatsworth, Georgia.

Tocharian culture, which designated a white-skinned people that thrived in 1500 BC. Many religious texts speak of white men or clans in places where the aboriginal people are dark skinned. The Book of Mormon refers to the Nephites, a group of men from Jerusalem who were early white American settlers (600 BC). The book of Enoch also hints that the biblical Noah was Caucasoid or maybe even albino.

However, there is another theory that these moon-eyed people were subterranean, like the famous cryptic "lizard people," or even that they were alien. If you consider many ancient cultures, such as the Egyptians, there are references to "sky people" with elongated skulls and large eyes. Even if you consider alien reports from modern day, alien skin is often pale, and their eyes are very large. Even more convincing is that most alien reports occur at night.

No matter who built the wall at Fort Mountain, the amazing feat of sojourning such an area with rocks that aren't even native to the area is something to be admired. It isn't known if the people were equipped with tools for the task or if their technology was above or equal to ours today. We might never know how the rocks got there and where they came from, but perhaps the mystery is what draws us to the wall in the first place.

Chapter Twenty-seven

THE CREEK WARS

One of the most important pieces of Alabama and Georgia history is the Creek Wars of 1812–13. Simplifying the war as Americans versus Native Americans is a misinterpretation, for it was much more complicated. It was not only a war between native and immigrant people but also a civil war of the Creek Nation, and it changed the presence of that people forever.

At one point, there was peace and justice between the Americans and the Creeks, and many believe that the Creeks had reason to continue living peacefully with the Americans. Many of the Creek Nation had begun to become more like the white men. They lived side by side with them; they were often visited by missionaries, and some began to worship the white men's God. They wore many of the same types of clothes, worked in settlers' fields and married white men or women. Because of the merging of the white man's culture with their own, the Creeks' tribal relations seemed to weaken. Many Creeks of mixed descent were in the Creek hierarchy. Frankly, it would not have taken many years of peace for the Creeks to become what settlers would call civilized instead of savage. Unfortunately for the Americans, savage was a misnomer, and they underestimated the cunning intelligence of the Creek Nation. That is where the trouble started.

What must be understood about the Creeks is that they were not just a tribe but a confederacy of tribes; they had their own empire with their own warriors, laws and establishments. When the Spanish encountered the Alabama Indians and began to fight them, the Alabama Creeks consented to an alliance with the Muscogee Creeks, creating the confederacy, and together, they fought against Cortés. They were shortly followed by the Tuckabatchee (some works write it Tookabatcha). This confederacy could be considered short-lived because, as with any alliance, it seems someone is always promoting schism.

The Creeks were given absolute title to their land by the Treaty of 1790, and the Americans helped defend it rigorously against trespassers. There were some who were opposed to this, such as the Spaniards who had settled there, claiming the land was theirs. At this time, Britain was still looking to regain the Americas and saw this hostility as a way to weaken the Americans. It launched thousands of emissaries to stir the hostility; one of its greatest was Tecumseh, a Shawnee warrior whose mission was twofold: one, stir the hostility for the British to gain their alliance, and two, unite an alliance with all natives against the whites.

Tecumseh studied the Americans. He saw their strength was in their union, and he witnessed them use the same men over and over to fight separate acting tribes and claim victory, thus weakening the native tribes. The Creeks were in a discord over a decision by the chiefs to allow a federal road through their land, and Tecumseh found it the right opportunity to visit the Great Council at Tuckabatchee in October 1811. Tecumseh was not new to the council. He had actually lived with the Creeks for two years, so when he returned, he was hailed by many as a hero of sorts, but not by all.

For days, Colonel Benjamin Hawkins, the Americans' ambassador, and the council waited to hear Tecumseh, but for days, he would say, "The sun is too far gone today; I will make my talk tomorrow." Because Tecumseh would not speak, Colonel Hawkins left, and when he did, Tecumseh made his speech. He told the Creeks they had made a grave mistake taking on the ways of the white man. He urged them to undress from white attire. He urged them to lose the ploughs that degraded them and made them slaves. He begged them to stop taking the arms of the white people, intermarrying and polluting the hierarchy with "half-blooded" men and women. He warned them the white man would cut down the forest and plant corn fields, build towns and make the rivers muddy washing their furrows, and when the Indians were weak enough and the whites strong enough, they would reduce the Indians to slaves, just as they did to the Africans.

Tecumseh believed the Great Spirit had given the land to the aboriginal people. He urged them to take up arms against the whites. He told them the Great Spirit was with them, that not one would be harmed and that their enemy would be crushed.

Once he made the great speech, he spent several days going to them in private, and he won many of them over, riling their ire against the Americans. However, he did not convince everyone. Many of the chiefs were against him. They had every reason to trust the white man. Many of them owned lots of land, and their families were mixed with whites. Basically, the Americans had made sure the chiefs were kept happy so as not to cause trouble. But one, Tustinnuggee Thlucco—or Big Warrior—roused Tecumseh's anger. He believed that a war with the whites would bring destruction on his nation, and he would not give in. Tecumseh said when he got back to Detroit, he would stomp his foot and all of Tuckabatchee would shake to the ground, a threat that many say was followed through with. As stated before in the black dog legend, most of Tuckabatchee was destroyed during the New Madrid earthquake.

Tecumseh did not give up, and he found many men with the same fire he had against the white man. One, whom he would call his second, was William "Red Eagle" Weatherford. William Weatherford was born to a Scotch trader from Georgia whose cunning intelligence and ambitious attitude he would pass to his son. But his mother was much more than that. She was a princess to the Creek Nation, born in the family of the Wind, the highest rank in the hierarchy of chieftains, and so, in turn, was Red Eagle. Red Eagle shared Tecumseh's hate for the white man. He believed with all his soul that the white man would be the undoing of the natives. His passion and rank were not the only things he brought to the table. As a man, Red Eagle was a wealthy trader and horse racer and held the interest of many of the Creeks with these races.

When Weatherford's enemies wrote about him—and it was only his enemies who wrote about him—while admiring his ability to lead troops to the equivalence of Andrew Jackson himself, their distaste for him was obvious. One wrote:

> Weatherford was born in the Creek nation. His father was an itinerant peddler, sordid, treacherous, and revengeful; his mother a full-blooded savage of the tribe of Seminoles. He partook of the bad qualities of both his parents and engrafted on the stock he inherited from others many that were peculiarly his own. With avarice, treachery, and a thirst for blood, he combines lust, gluttony, and a devotion to every species of criminal carousal.

This was the underestimation Tecumseh was looking for in a leader. He knew the white man would think Weatherford too savage to compete, and so he trusted Red Eagle with his men in the South while Tecumseh went north on his mission. Due to Red Eagle's new influence, many of the Creek Nation became hostile and were ready for war, especially the Alabamas, to whom Red Eagle's influence was almost unending. After a group of Tecumseh's men, led by Little Warrior, killed seven American families and took a woman named Mrs. Crawley hostage in the spring of 1812, the Americans wanted justice. The band of warriors were sought out and put to death, which roused the warring Creeks, often called Red Sticks, even more. Murders became frequent, and there was civil unrest between the "peacefuls" (the Creeks who would not fight the Americans) and the Red Sticks.

Big Warrior sent a message to Red Eagle's men saying, "You are but a few Alabama people. You say the Great Spirit visits you frequently; that he comes in the sun, and speaks to you; that the sun comes down just above your head. Now we want to see and hear what you have heard. Let us have the same proof, and then we will believe. You have nothing to fear; the people who did the killing on the Ohio are put to death, and the law is satisfied." He was answered when they killed Big Warrior's messenger, and thus, the civil war among the Creeks began. Many would fight with the white man against their warring brothers, and it seemed, at least to Red Eagle, that this was not the war he was meant to fight.

He attempted to abandon his men when he found he would have to fight his brother Jack Weatherford and his half brother David Tait, not to mention the fighting endangered his sweetheart, Lucy Cornell. However, when he returned home, the Creeks had seized his children and his slaves and threatened to kill his children if he faltered from their cause. So boldly, he stayed loyal to the Red Sticks.

After the Battle of Burnt Corn, which the Creeks lost, the white man could have gained a foothold, yet they only half attempted to meet hostility with any aggression. Their only tactic was to fortify some bastions, such as Fort Mims and Fort Glass. During this time, America was also at war with Great Britain, and many chose to ally with one side or another. Red Eagle wanted to burn part of the Creek territory in Mobile to avoid more bloodshed, yet unless they attacked outside the Creek territory, allied leaders did not have the authority to permit it, thus turning the fury of the warring Creeks against Fort Mims, which was a massacre. The Americans knew if the Choctaws and Chickasaws joined forces with the warring Creeks, they would stand no chance against the combined force, especially after the massacre at Fort Mims; however, to their surprise, Choctaw chief Pushmatahaw came to the Americans first. He said in Choctaw council that Tecumseh was a bad man. He pointed out how many of the Choctaws' white friends were killed by the warring Creeks at Mims, and he joined forces against them. The tide was turning for the Creeks. They hunted the white man like deer, yet they were soon to be the prey. The fiercest and most energetic Indian fighter was coming to rectify the state of affairs for the Americans: Andrew Jackson.

"We are about to furnish these savages a lesson of admonition. We are about to teach them that our long forbearance has not proceeded from an insensibility of wrongs or an inability to redress them. They stand in need of such warning," said Jackson.

Jackson headed south very sick and wounded from a gunfight. He was so sick that he had to be helped on his horse by his men. He came to the cause with just volunteers. The Tennessee volunteers were a hindrance to Jackson; they arrived very few in number and with little supplies. The War Department was not aware of how formidable an opponent Jackson was fighting, and Red Eagle and his men were gaining in numbers and were "whipping Jackson" all over the place.

Then, Jackson got what he wanted: an army five thousand troops strong, plus the alliance with the Choctaws. He was ready for a battle; he had wind in his sails and was headed toward Tohopeka, or the Horse Shoe, now called Horse Shoe Bend in Alabama. The Red Sticks there were only about a thousand strong, plus their women and children, but the stronghold was almost impenetrable.

Many writers of the time thought that Indians would not create fortresses, that they were more offensive in nature. But they also said that Red Eagle was more than just an Indian. He was also a white man and, essentially, was civilized. He was trained by General Alexander McGillivray and General Le Clerc Milfort; he had learned fortification by visiting Mobile, and he was ready for a defensive hold.

Finally, on March 27, 1814, Jackson and the Red Sticks would meet face to face. The Red Sticks were led by Menawa, first called Hothlepoya, or Great Warrior. (Red Eagle was not present at the battle of the Horse Shoe.) Posting troops on a hill and his Indian forces in the stream, Jackson made sure they left no gap. The cannons were dreadfully exposed, but his men were brave and held their ground. They fired with little avail; they could not penetrate the wall built to fortify the village of Tohopeka. John Coffee, one of Jackson's men and his nephew by marriage, was anxious to prevent any escapes while holding ground at the river. He and their allied Cherokee forces made a distraction at the river, setting fire to the homes along the back side of the shoe. Soon, they were face to face with the enemy, attacking from the rear, and the Creeks fought fiercely. They would not be taken captive

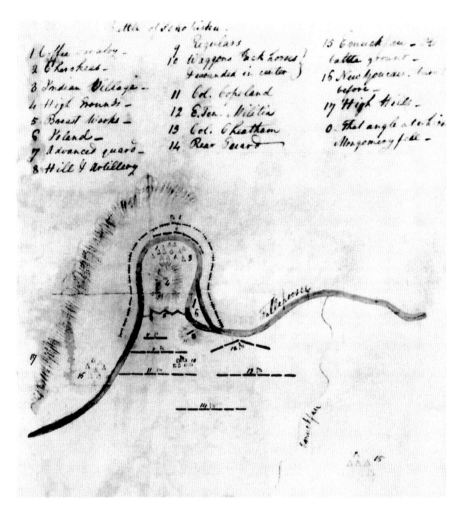

A replica of the map of the Horse Shoe drawn by Andrew Jackson on display at Horse Shoe Bend National Military Park.

and would only surrender to death. This did spook the Americans because the battle became butchery, a massacre of sorts; yet little by little, the Creeks were driven, bloodied and broken, to the riverbank, where the remnant of them made their last stand. When the bloody battle ended, 557 Creeks were dead, plus the 300 who had tried to swim away but were shot in the water and sank. So many were killed in the river that it ran red with blood for a week after the battle.

The power of the Creeks was destroyed at Tohopeka. Most of their warriors were killed, save Menawa, who lay badly wounded among the dead until nightfall, when he escaped by cover of darkness. The women and children were left poor and hungry in the woods or arrested by Jackson's men. The Red Sticks were beaten, and Red Eagle felt he had no choice but to surrender. Mounting his gray horse, he loaded his gun. He thought about Big Warrior and how, if he had the chance, he would kill him. Seeing a deer, he shot it and loaded it on the back of his horse. He arrived at Fort Jackson to surrender. Meeting Big Warrior, Red Eagle told him, "You traitor! If you give me any insolence I will blow a ball through your cowardly heart." He would have, too, had General Jackson not stopped him.

He begged that Jackson go find the starving women and children and care for them and that he would give his life for theirs. While others shouted, "Kill him! Kill him!" Jackson silently said, "Any man who would kill as brave a man as this would rob the dead." He invited Red Eagle for a drink, and they negotiated his surrender. Jackson offered protection to Red Eagle, although Big Warrior tried to kill him despite Jackson's orders. Because the thirst by the peaceful Creeks for Red Eagle's blood was so strong, he was protected to the point that he lived with Andrew Jackson for several years at Jackson's home.

A peace treaty was signed August 9, 1814, by which the Creeks gave up the southern part of their territory. The purpose was to keep the Creeks from bad advisors, any lingering Tecumseh followers (for he had fallen in battle in October 1813) and the Spanish to the south in Pensacola, Florida. By these means, Jackson made it nearly impossible for war to begin again.

Red Eagle established himself as a trader in Alabama, and he mostly abandoned that name. William Weatherford died of exhaustion during a bear hunt on March 9, 1824. He had many children who intermarried with whites and extinguished all traces of Indian blood in his descendants. Despite the friendship that he and Andrew Jackson seemed to have, it did not quell the hatred that Jackson seemed to feel toward native people. Due to Jackson's drive to "rid" the South of the Indian, the Creek people never again rose to the empirical state they had possessed before. If anything, the Red Sticks solidified Americans' growing hatred of the Indian people, and they would prove to aid in the undoing of the entire southern Indian population.

Chapter Twenty-eight

INDIAN REMOVAL

Once Andrew Jackson had all but rid most of Alabama and Georgia of the Creeks, he turned his attention to the Cherokees. There was much going on in the nation during the Creek Wars and after. There were treaties being made by the Creeks and Cherokees that made the Americans nervous. There was also a growing hatred for Indians, not to mention the land race of who would control Alabama and Georgia's prime cultivating land (popularly known in Alabama as "Alabama Fever").

Five or six million acres of the best lands in Georgia were in the Indian territories, not to mention gold, gold and more gold. Also, Pensacola, Florida, possessed an extraordinary advantage as a seaport and would be a commercial rival to Mobile, Alabama, and New Orleans, Louisiana. As always in the South, cotton was king, and growers knew that five hundred acres of cotton could yield up to $6,000 a year, which was a substantial amount of money at that time, and by 1816, ten thousand "squatters" (white and Spanish settlers in Indian Territory) had entered the territories, popularly called the "Garden of America."

President Andrew Jackson was not innocent of this land greed. He had an interest in the South Tennessee River area of Alabama known as Muscle Shoals because it was prime cotton land. He had his nephew by marriage, John Coffee, elected head government surveyor of the Alabama land cession so they knew exactly where the most profitable land was. Jackson attempted the presidency in 1824 and succeeded in 1829. He passed the Indian Removal Act in 1830 and tried for years to persuade or force tribes to "voluntarily" give up their territories. At his death in 1845, he had his home in Tennessee, the Hermitage, along with two plantations, 161 slaves, a stable of fifty horses and hundreds of head of livestock.

Half-blooded Indians were cashing in as well. By 1819, the Cherokee population was about 15,000, one-third of whom lived west of the Mississippi River. The eastern nation was 13,563 with another 300 estimated married to whites and 1,200 who were slaves. They had large herds of cattle, horses, hogs and sheep. They grew cotton, tobacco, wheat and apple and peach orchards. They sold butter, cheese and even clothes and nearly all merchants were Cherokee. The truth is, the whites weren't scared of the native Indians' savagery but of their civilization.

The Cherokees had even met at New Echota on July 26, 1827, to adopt a national constitution. John Ross, a half-blooded Cherokee, was the president of the convention. Charles R. Hicks was the principal chief, and Ross was the assistant chief. In 1828, Nunnatsunega, or White Path, headed a rebellion near present-day Ellijay, Georgia, against the new laws. His followers, much like the warring Creeks during the Creek Wars, were known as the Red Sticks; however, they did not succeed, and John Ross became principal chief by 1828.

With this constitution, the Cherokees claimed the right to govern themselves independently of Georgia or the U.S. government. The U.S.

The homes in modern Eufaula, Alabama, show little evidence of past Indian occupants of the land.

government claimed the right of enforcing its laws on the government of the Indian tribes, and Georgia's own laws were in conflict with both the Cherokee and the U.S. governments' laws.

After the Cherokee constitution was passed, Georgia passed a resolution that it "had the power and the right to possess herself, by any means she might choose, of lands in dispute, and to extend over them her authority and laws." Basically, Georgia made a move against the Cherokees saying it would take their land if it wanted to and exert its own laws there. A great deal of this attitude had to do with the 1829 gold fever along the Dahlonega Gold Belt in Georgia.

One Georgia man who was instrumental to what happened to the Cherokees was Wilson Lumpkin. Lumpkin was at different times in his career a U.S. representative, a senator and also a Georgia governor. He sought to "relieve Georgia from the encumbrance of her Indian population, and at the same time benefit the Indians." It was Lumpkin's idea to relocate the Cherokees to a centralized location. His autobiography suggests that he truly believed he was helping the Indians. He "wished to place them in a permanent home where the missionary efforts of all pious and good men, Churches and Christian associates, might have a permanent field of labor, to carry out their good designs of Christianizing and civilizing a most interesting heathen people." He even extended his "hopes to the day when Indian people might become an interesting and worthy member of our great confederacy of states." While he wrote these words with seemingly noble intentions, his feelings toward the civility of the Cherokees were clear. When President John Q. Adams appointed him as part of the Committee of Indian Affairs, he quickly had a hands-off approach, as if to say, "I never thought he would take me so seriously."

Lumpkin was just one in a long line of people who feared or hated Indians. It is often said that which we fear, we will quickly hate, and this was exactly what happened to the Indian peoples all over the South.

The December 20, 1828 resolution for Indian removal took effect June 1, 1830, when the entire Cherokee Nation was annexed to 160-acre reservations in Georgia, with no deeds to the land, and their remaining there was completely up to the Georgia legislature. The resolution stated no Indian could bring suit on a white man, dig up gold on his own land or hold seats in council. The Americans passed any law that would make it uncomfortable for the Cherokees to live east of the Mississippi. Frankly, the Indians were treated much like an Alabama mosquito, a bloody nuisance, and the Americans were all resolved for their annihilation.

By February 1835, two parties from the Cherokees went to Washington to resolve the issue. One party was headed by John Ross, who still wanted to fight for the Cherokee land, and the other by Major John Ridge, who was ready to negotiate for Indian removal. During the Ridge Treaty, Reverend J.F. Schermerhorn offered payment of $4.5 million to the Cherokees for all their land east of the Mississippi River. It was rejected and a counter offer of $20 million was proposed. Shermerhorn rejected this offer and signed the Ridge Treaty for $4.5 million on March 14, 1835, but it had the expressed stipulation that it must be approved by the Cherokee Nation in full council assembly before it could be considered a binding force. It was rejected in October 1835 by the Cherokee Nation.

The council authorized a delegation headed by John Ross to conclude a treaty; however, before its departure, Ross was arrested at his home in Tennessee (where he had moved to escape life threats) and held without charge or apology. It was an obvious ploy to keep him from the council. At the same time, the *Cherokee Phoenix* newspaper was suppressed as well as many members of council. When the treaty was signed in for the Cherokees' removal, only three to five hundred men, women and children from the Cherokee Nation were in attendance, and none were officers of the Cherokee Nation. The treaty was signed on December 29, 1835.

The removal was to be paid for by the U.S. government and was to be conducted within two years of the sign date of the treaty. When Ross was released, he appealed the treaty, claiming fraud, but it was to no avail. General Wool, who was put in charge of the removal, rejected the idea that this was a solemn treaty. He knew it was fraudulent and wrote to President Jackson. He said the Cherokees were in a very poor state. He said they would not eat or take a handout from the U.S. government, that many had had no more than sap from the root of a tree for days and that some of them said they would die first. He begged the president to reconsider, stating they would all go penniless to the West. His letter did no one any good. Only two thousand of the nearly fifteen thousand had gone voluntarily to the West.

The Cherokees had been disarmed by General Wool in 1839. Despite the treaty, many of the Cherokees refused to believe the removal would actually happen. The believed it too much of a burden on the government or that some other arrangement could be made. They were sorely mistaken. Seven thousand troops showed up to rip them from their spinning wheels, schools and stores. They were chased through the caves and mountains of Georgia and dragged to the valley, some dead, few alive. They were lined up as slaves and set out, a few by steamboat and about thirteen thousand by land. They left in October 1839, and it took them six months to travel to the West, near present-day Oklahoma. Many died of sickness, but more died of sadness. White Path died along the way as well as John Ross's wife; more than four thousand Cherokees died along the Trail of Tears. Many would say that the removal of the Cherokees was one of the cruelest and saddest acts carried out by the U.S. government.

By this time, it was clear that the prediction of the Creek Nation had come true. Much of the forests of the South were cut down and brought under cultivation. The land was robbed of its precious minerals in the gold rush of 1829. The rivers were muddied with industry and pollution, the Chattahoochee River being one of the most polluted rivers. Even today, the Chattahoochee is in great peril because of pollution. The Indian nations had fallen from their pinnacles. They were broken and beaten, forced out and robbed.

Indian removal happened all over the South. In Louisiana, the Houma Choctaw Indians were forced into what could be considered uninhabitable lands. The Seminole in Florida were forced to do the same. The Creeks were all but annihilated in Alabama and Georgia, and the Chickasaws were forced to Oklahoma from Mississippi. The remaining Indians were forced into agreements or treaties much like the Cherokees were. These tribes were named the "Five Civilized Tribes." Most of the Indians in the South were forced to join one of these nations to be called Indian and be given severance by the U.S. government, commonly referred to by many as "Indian money." Those who refused were forced out by any and all means necessary, even murder.

Many of the Native Americans lost their autonomy and their heritage during and after the Indian removal. Even when they got to Oklahoma, they were penniless and had to fight just to prove they were Indian for set-up money from the government. Many claims were rejected and then later reopened. It was the belief that the two men responsible for accepting claims were purposely rejecting them to save the United States money. Many starved and died or were forced into concentration camps. Later, by the 1920s and 1930s, Indians began to leave the reservations. They lied on their census reports, claiming they were European immigrants, and stopped receiving help from the government. It was a common conception that if you were Indian, there stood a chance the government would take your land; therefore, people began to lie about who they were.

It is a known fact that the Indian removal left a scar on America and Indians. It is one of the bloodiest and most shameful times in American history. Some see that history repeating itself. Perhaps it is less bloody, but it is nonetheless shameful. Indians still fight for autonomy today; even as late as 1990, the Seminole negotiated for land in Florida. Many mixed-blood Indians fight to claim their heritage, meeting great resistance from full-blooded Indians. It is no wonder that there is mistrust to those of mixed race or any trace of white blood, considering many half-blooded or mixed-descent leaders failed or betrayed them during the 1800s. Those wounds are still fresh because they have remained open, constantly bleeding, with no end in sight.

Chapter Twenty-nine

THE FIRES AND FURY OF THE CIVIL WAR ALONG THE CHATTAHOOCHEE

D uring the goings-on of the Indian Removal Act, America was fighting another battle, a battle of independence—not revolutionary independence, but a more internal independence between federal government and the state. Statehood had always been supreme and sovereign, but much like the Native Americans attempted to declare their sovereignty, the states struggled to remain under their own authority. Jefferson Davis wrote in retrospect of the Civil War:

> *The object of this work has been from historical data to show that the Southern States had rightfully the power to withdraw from a Union into which they had, as sovereign communities, voluntarily entered; that the denial of that right was a violation of the letter and spirit of the compact between the States; and that the war waged by the Federal Government against the seceding States was in a disregard of the limitations of the Constitution, and destructive of the principles of the Declaration of Independence.*

Although Davis claimed that slavery had nothing to do with the cause of the war, it was, in fact, the greatest cause of the war.

In 1619, a Dutch vessel brought to America over twenty African slaves to be held in bondage. This was the beginning of the slave trade. The importation of slaves had been abolished in January 1808 in an overall unanimous decision between the states. However, the question arose if a man could go with his slaves to a new territory where the non-slaveholder could go with his property of any sort, and the South did not believe that the federal government had the right to decide that for them. Davis was very clear that the term "extension of slavery" never meant adding more slaves to the South or opening up the slave trade again but rather when and where the slaves already owned could go.

It was obvious slavery was the teetering point on which the Union stood. States entered into the Union as either a freed state or a slave state. By 1840, there was so much bitterness between the two sides of the issue that threats of seceding became as common as a child's temper tantrum. When the abolitionists got involved, the endeavor to stir up the Northern ire against the South (to the tune of zealous harassment) and encourage slaves to revolt was quite damaging to efforts of reconciliation. Abolitionists felt strongly that the Union should drive out the Southern states if they refused to abolish slavery, even by purging them with fire for their sins. Their acts and words were extreme.

On October 16, 1859, John Brown, a radical abolitionist, and his supporters descended on the town of Harpers Ferry. They captured prominent citizens and seized the federal armory and arsenal in hopes the slaves would raid and revolt. Colonel Robert E. Lee and troops killed many raiders and captured Brown. He was sentenced to death for treason against Virginia, murder and slave insurrection and hanged on December 2, 1859. His actions put Southern states on guard; they were quickly becoming the enemy of the Union. It was already Southern opinion that Congress was insulting the South because it held slaves. To the average Southerner, prejudice and hatred for the South was running deeper by the minute.

Southerners also believed their interests were burdened with tax for the benefit of the North with the new slave tariff. With the cultivation of cotton, slave labor was much more prominent in the South, and they believed the Union expected them to foot the bills. Southerners asked for reprieve and threatened secession. When Republican Abraham Lincoln won the presidential election, the South withdrew its representatives from Congress and its states from the Union.

Davis and others sought peaceful separation, so a peace conference was held, to which representatives of the states were invited. Measure after measure was proposed to avoid war, and all were rejected by the Union. These rejections solidified the Southern opinion that the Union believed the recusant states must be whipped back into submission. Though it was never an admitted fact, considering the amount of money the Union would lose by losing exports of cotton and other agricultural products of the South, they

Modern-day Columbus, Georgia's Chattahoochee River.

had a vested interest in reclaiming the South, and pride was on the menu as well.

On February 4, 1861, delegates from Virginia, Arkansas, Florida, Georgia, North Carolina, South Carolina, Mississippi, Texas, Louisiana, Alabama and Tennessee met in Montgomery, Alabama, to create the new capital of the Confederacy. President Jefferson Davis was inaugurated at the statehouse in Montgomery on February 18 and again in Richmond, Virginia, on February 22. From the very beginning, the cloud of war loomed.

On April 27 of that same year, President Lincoln declared war on the Confederate States of America after the Confederates' attempt to overtake Fort Sumter. War went on through much of the Southern states for the next three years, and by September 1, 1864, Atlanta had fallen to Union forces led by General William Tecumseh Sherman, his name paying homage to the great Shawnee warrior Tecumseh. General Sherman served under General Ulysses Grant in 1862 and 1863 during his campaigns in Mississippi and Tennessee.

Sherman was known as a crafty and fierce leader. Fidgety and impatient, he broke down from pressure so often the papers labeled him insane. Sherman laughed and claimed, "I'm too red-haired to be patient." There was one thing Sherman was not impatient about, and that was the "art of war." He likened war to a storm and had the skill and knowledge to generate that storm. Using the destructive power of a storm, Sherman decimated much of the South.

Sherman commanded nearly 100,000 troops based around Chattanooga, Tennessee. He confronted a Confederate force of about 64,000 led by Joseph Johnston whose sole task was to block Federal penetration into Georgia, no doubt by holding the Chattahoochee River, the Chattahoochee being the last major geographical barrier between the Federal army and the city of Atlanta. Johnston did not succeed. Sherman took Atlanta on September 1, 1864.

Prior to the siege, in July 1864, Sherman sent cavalry under Major General Lovell H. Rousseau to lead a campaign into Alabama, often referred to as Rousseau's Raid. Rousseau's duties were to destroy the railroad from Montgomery, Alabama, to Atlanta, Georgia, cutting off supplies to Confederate troops defending Atlanta. The Montgomery and West Point Railroad was a vital supply line for munitions and war materials to General Joe Johnston. With 2,500 troops, Rousseau burned and destroyed nearly thirty, very important, miles of Southern railways. Beginning in Loachapoka, Alabama, located in now Lee County, Rousseau's men burned and melted the railways through Loachapoka, Notasulga, Auburn and Opelika, capturing a train headed to Atlanta with Confederate supplies.

When Rousseau's Raid was finished, nearly all of Lee County was burned. In Opelika alone, Rousseau confiscated 4,200 pounds of bacon, flour and sugar, as well as six railroad freight cars filled with leather. He had covered nearly four hundred miles of Alabama and left fire and fury in his wake, destroying a large chunk of the state. Rousseau and his men joined Sherman on his siege of Atlanta.

A month before Sherman claimed, "Atlanta is ours and fairly won," the Union navy had taken control of Mobile Bay. Sherman's next move was a forward one. He first wanted to turn Atlanta into an armed camp; however, Union forces were dependent on a single railroad line running north to Federal supply depots in Tennessee. He considered a joint operation with Union forces operating out of New Orleans to capture Columbus, Georgia. Columbus sat on the Chattahoochee River and was the site of the Confederates' most productive arsenals. With Columbus and a connection south to a supply source secured, Sherman imagined a thrust farther into central Georgia; he would change courses from Columbus.

On September 29, 1864, Confederate general John B. Hood and his Tennessee forces began to march counterclockwise around Atlanta. By October 3, his infantry was wrecking the Federal depots at Acworth and Big Shanty on Sherman's supply line.

Sherman reacted with a letter to Grant that said, "Until we can repopulate Georgia, it is useless to occupy it, but the utter destruction of its railroads, houses, and people will cripple its military resources. By attempting to hold the rail we lose a thousand men monthly and will gain no result. I can make the march and make Georgia howl." Sherman had made a decision: destroy Atlanta and all of Georgia. Sherman was determined to leave Georgia a barren wasteland.

Sherman would use a template he used in the raid on Vicksburg to Meridian, Mississippi. While Hood veered westward to Gaylesville, Alabama, on the Georgia border, Sherman stood in wait to see if he would return. In two days, he had not wavered from his westward course, so Sherman sent a telegraph to Lincoln's military chief of staff: "I now consider myself authorized to execute my plan to destroy the railroad from Chattanooga to Atlanta and strike out into the heart of Georgia, and make for Charleston, Savannah, or on the mouth of the Apalachicola River."

On Saturday, November 12, Sherman ordered Orlando M. Poe to destroy the city of Atlanta's railroads, depots, steam machineries, etc: "But be careful not to use fire, which would endanger other buildings than those set apart for destruction." Poe and his men were good at what they did. Despite Sherman's orders, as they were destroying Atlanta, fire burst out on the opposite side of town somewhere on the Chattanooga railroad. The same day, the bridge across the Chattahoochee was smashed. North of the river, the town of Acworth suffered the same fate as the cities of Rome, Kingston and Cartersville. One Ohio commander stated, "Our soldiers are determined to burn, plunder, and destroy everything in their way on this march."

Even many of the Union commanders were shocked at the amount of vandalism. They burned everything in sight: stations, towns, rails, depots, cotton mills, artilleries and even homes. For miles as far as the eye could see were blazing fires. At any one time, Sherman had up to six columns going in different directions, burning, plundering and pillaging as they went. The Union forces were throwing food, clothes and other supplies in the streets before it burned.

Sherman seemed unfazed by the scene. An Ohio officer from the Fourteenth Corps added, "I saw Gen. Sherman walking the streets of the blazing city paying no heed to the flames. I don't believe he has any mercy in his composition." Sherman once said to Major Henry Hitchcock, "There are men who do this. Set as many guards as you please, they will slip in and set fire. I never ordered burning of any dwelling—didn't order this, but can't be helped. I say Jeff Davis burnt them." Captain Poe felt the same as Sherman; he stated, "For military purposes the city of Atlanta has ceased to exist."

The Confederate troops were just as guilty of destruction, setting fires to bridges they crossed, destroying railways and setting up bastions and blockades across roadways. General Hood advised Wheeler's cavalry, "If Sherman advances to the South or East, destroy all things in front that might be useful to him, and keep a portion of your force constantly destroying his trains." Wheeler's cavalry burned up corn and fodder, driving the stocks for ten miles on each side of the railroads and twenty-five miles to the right and rear of Sherman's forces.

Creating destruction moving toward Macon, Georgia, Sherman had the Confederates convinced he would try to take Macon, and Confederate general Beauregard concentrated many troops there. General Richard Taylor was convinced that "Macon was the safest place in Georgia." Truthfully, Sherman had no intentions of taking Macon but moved toward Milledgeville and on to Savannah, burning Fayette, Clayton, Henry and Butts Counties as he went.

The lack of focus of Confederate commanders in Central Georgia was a benefit to Sherman's operation. In many ways, it was the key to his success. Three cities under Sherman's shadow reacted differently to the looming threat of siege. Augusta was confident; Charleston was near panic; and Savannah had a tone of self-reliance.

Because Savannah all but surrendered to Sherman, it was spared much of the destruction that occurred in the South, and Savannah welcomed Sherman into its bosom, no doubt to save its crops and way of life; Savannah's socialites bluffed quite well. For Sherman, the Savannah break was a time to savor his accomplishments and decide his next move. This was in December 1864.

General Sherman's March to the Sea was a military success, but it was the downfall for the old ways of the South. Families were penniless and out on the streets. In Atlanta alone, thousands of people died in trenches where they lived for six weeks while Atlanta burned. Some said that "not even a crow flapped" over the smoldering city.

As a side note, the city of Columbus, Georgia, was not spared. James H. Wilson led a raid of his own while Confederate troops were busy with Sherman. With 13,480 cavalry troops, Wilson's blitzkrieg ran from Montevallo and Birmingham (at that time Elyton) down to Selma and Montgomery and then over to Columbus. Although nearly six months after Sherman changed courses, much of Columbus was destroyed or taken by March 1865, almost an afterthought of the war, since by April 1865, General Lee had surrendered, President Lincoln had been assassinated and the war had officially ended. Wilson had "taken the last great Confederate storehouse" with Columbus. What they did not take militarily, they destroyed. The CSS *Jackson* was one of the largest ironclad ships built in the South. It was 225 feet long, 54 feet wide and weighed 2,000 tons. It was dockside on the Chattahoochee River when Wilson took Columbus. It was set ablaze to prevent any later use by Confederates. It was set adrift down the Chattahoochee completely engulfed in flames. It burned for two weeks before sinking to the bottom of the Chattahoochee where it sat for ninety-five years. It was raised in 1961 by citizens during a Civil War Centennial. A little-known secret is that they used dynamite to loosen it from the bottom. It now has a resting home at the Civil War Naval Museum at Port Columbus in Columbus, Georgia.

In 1936–38, what became known as *The Slave Narrative* collection was compiled in seventeen states and consists of more than two thousand interviews with former slaves. It allowed these people to tell their stories so that others could hear what slavery was like firsthand. It has been considered controversial to even use these narratives from a historical standpoint because some question their authenticity and reliability; however, it was the last opportunity to interview a former slave, most of the subjects being in their nineties or over one hundred. It was also the last opportunity to listen to and learn from these few remaining souls.

While most of the stories had a scripted amount of questions—such as how old were you when you were freed, do you go to church and what do you remember about the war—some tales are just for fun and give us a full peek inside the old superstitions and stories of African American culture, which has now become the basis for many of our legends today.

Each subject interviewed in Alabama and Georgia was asked if he or she remembers the Yankees coming to town. Below are many eyewitness recollections from freed slaves along the Chattahoochee and those entwined with Sherman's March to the Sea, including Rousseau's Raid (with modern verbiage so as to be less confusing and/or offensive):

CORNELIA ROBINSON

Opelika, Alabama

Cornelia Robinson was four when the Yankees came through. She likened them to a hurricane:

> *The Yankees came through and cleaned out the smokehouse even left the lard bucket as clean as your hand. Old Master took his best horses and mules*

to the big swamp, and the Yankees couldn't find them. But they tore up everything they couldn't take with them. They poured all the syrup out, and it ran down the road like water. One little poor boy was so scared that he went out and got up the cows, and when he couldn't find some of them, he laid down in a hollow stump and nearly froze to death; he wasn't "no count for nothing" after that. The misses saved all her jewels and such from the Yankees. She brought them to the cabins and hid them amongst us.

FRANK SMITH, NINETY

Birmingham, Alabama

I was born in old 'Ginny [Virginia], *and my old master was doctor constable; and he and us all lived out a piece from Norfolk where you can see the whole ocean. Old master died eight years before the big war, and old missus refugee down to Alexandria where her mammy and pappy lived. I was the house boy* [sic] *in old missus['s] pappy's house. When the big war started, old missus took me and her children and refugee down somewhere that was a courthouse, what they called Culpepper, and we lived in town with some kinfolks. The soldiers marched right in front of our house by the front gate, and they was going to Harper's Ferry to kill old John Brown who was killing white folks and freeing slaves for their time. That was Mister Lincoln's job after the war. And no slaves wanted to be free until then. We lived close to the hotel where General Lee and a whole passel of soldiers stayed, and they had the shiniest clothes I ever saw. They were fine gentlemen; and the old missus, she let me wait on them whilst she didn't need me to work around the house, and they give me a dime. I shined General Lee's shoes sometimes and he always gives me a dime and said, "That looks nice." He was straight and dignified and didn't talk much, but he walked up and down in the front gallery and ordered to bring him telegraphs from Bull Run while us and the Yankees were fighting. Lawrdy Mercy, I heard them talking about "bull run" that day, and I thought somebody's bull had got out and we and the Yankees was trying to catch him and get him back in the pasture. The missus sold me when I broke a knife handle and the new master wasn't like my own white folks. I joined the Yankee army and got a job working for a captain named Esserton, him and lieutenant somebody. We followed General Sherman clear to Atlanta and ten miles further on and marched clear back to Chattanooga and then kept on 'til we got to Nashville. I was sure glad to get away from Atlanta because there were dead men every way you looked after they quit fighting. They gave me a uniform, but I didn't get no gun; I fought with a frying pan. We stayed in Nashville a while, and when the war was over, Captain Esserton wanted to take me to Illinois with him and give me a job. But I didn't like those Yankees. They wanted you to work all the time, and that's something I hadn't been brought up to do. They turned me free, and I went with a passel of General Lee's soldiers who were going home; and we went down and crossed the biggest river I ever saw.*

William Ward, 105

Atlanta, Georgia

When Sherman reached the present site of Hapeville, he bombarded Atlanta with cannon, afterwards marching through and burning the city. The white residents made all sorts of frantic attempts to hide their money and other valuables. Some hiding places were under stumps of trees and in sides of hills. Incidentally Sherman's army found quite a bit of the hidden wealth. At the time Sherman marched through Atlanta, ward and other slaves were living in an old mansion at the present site of Peachtree and Baker Streets. He says that Sherman took him and his fellow slaves as far as Virginia to carry powder and shot to the soldiers. He didn't know if Sherman planned on keeping him in slavery or freeing him. He remembers when Atlanta was just a few hills without any buildings.

Even today, southerners suffer from the destruction of the war. It took years to rebuild much of the South, and all will say it never again saw the glory it once had. Our "antiques" only go back to the 1930s, where in the North you are more likely to find a piece from colonial times. Several members of the older generation hold on to everything they have because their belief is you are more prone to lose it living in the South. Southerners are quickly labeled as stubborn, prejudiced and unintelligent. Many have heard it said if you open your mouth and have a southern accent, people will count ten points off your IQ.

It is common for a southerner to have a chip on his shoulder about the "War of Northern Aggression," and it's no wonder. Some say those who fought for the South did it for the same reasons our forefathers fought for independence; they fought against tyranny. Others say those who fought for the South did it for selfish greed and insolence. No matter the cause, the fires and furies of the Civil War remain aflame still, over 150 years later.

Chapter Thirty

HORACE KING

The Greatest Architect History Forgot to Mention

African American history is an integral part of American history. Some of the greatest minds came to this country as slaves or were born into slavery. These men and women were inventors, scientists, abolitionists and even revolutionists. They were more than just something we celebrate in February of each year, and they were definitely much more than the shallow graves with no markers we buried them in, remembered by no one and forgotten by all. One of these great minds is only remembered in a small corner of the world, and barely even there. His love and gratitude were marked but not on his own grave. It seems school history books forgot to mention his genius, skill and aptitude. History left out this man, Horace King, and the example he set for real men—men of honor.

Horace King was born in South Carolina in 1807. Little is said about King's childhood. It seems he only became of historical importance when he started building bridges. His father was a mulatto named Edmund King, and his mother, Susan (also called Lucky), was the daughter of a Catawba Indian and an African slave woman. He was, like many of these important souls, born into slavery. When his master died in 1829, he and his mother became the property of John Godwin, a South Carolina builder and bridge contractor.

In early 1830, Columbus, Georgia, was one of the largest raw border towns scattered along the Chattahoochee River, and on the other side of the river was Creek Indian territory. When the land was ceded in 1832 during the Creek Wars, the opening for westward expansion began. When Columbus

Many of King's bridges have been replaced for safety reasons within the last twenty years, thus adding to the demise of his legend.

began to expand, city officials advertised for bids for a bridge across the Chattahoochee to the newly ceded territories, and John Godwin quickly bid on the project. His bid was accepted in March 1832, and Godwin and King moved to Columbus to erect the first public bridge connecting Alabama to Georgia. When completed, the nine-hundred-foot-long covered bridge, designed in the Town truss mode (after Ithiel Town, Connecticut architect and colleague of Godwin's). Quickly, both Godwin and King's reputations as master bridge builders soared.

It was clear from the beginning that King was more of a junior partner than a slave to Godwin. King was the supervisor on construction for his bridges. Together, they built bridges at Irwinton (now Eufaula, Alabama); West Point, Georgia; Tallassee, Alabama; and Florence, Alabama. Godwin guaranteed his bridges for five years even against flood. During March 1841, a flood swept away the entire City Bridge in Columbus and was replaced the same year, further solidifying the skills of King's ingenuity.

King's genius took Godwin far, and bridges were not his only feat. King worked on mills, courthouses and even homes. His skills became such a commodity that people claimed he built their homes or their bridges even when he did not. Even Robert Jemison Jr. of Tuscaloosa, state senator, took notice. Godwin and King had several joint ventures with Jemison, including bridges, sawmills and other construction projects all over Tuscaloosa. King even worked on Bryce Mental Institution in Tuscaloosa, an architectural treasure of the area.

In 1839, King married Frances Thomas, the daughter of a free woman named Molly. They had four sons and one daughter who all worked in the family business. By 1846, Godwin began to suffer financial setbacks and realized King could be taken to settle debts. Godwin arranged for Robert Jemison to petition the Alabama General Assembly for King's freedom. He succeeded, and King was freed on February 3, 1846.

During the next decade, King continued to prosper architecturally, working with Jemison and Godwin. Godwin and King remained close. When Godwin died in 1859, King had a Masonic monument erected over Godwin's grave. The inscription reads:

> *Born Oct. 17, 1798. Died Feb. 26, 1859.*
> *This stone was placed here by Horace King,*
> *In lasting remembrance of the love and gratitude*
> *He felt for his lost friend and former master.*

At Godwin's death, King quietly provided for Godwin's children, making them his wards out of the love he had for Godwin. When Godwin's daughter, Mary, married William Penn C. Yonge just before Godwin's death, the Gothic-style cottage of Spring Villa in Opelika, Alabama, was built for them. Most claims say King built the house as a wedding present to Mary.

During the Civil War, although a self-proclaimed Unionist, King worked for the Confederacy, erecting blockades and a rolling mill. Records from 1863 and 1864 show King supplied logs, treenails, large oak beams, oak knees and 15,630 board feet of lumber for the CSS *Jackson*. It was a hard time for King, losing his wife in 1864 and trying to hold Godwin's family operations together. He also had problems with Federal troops stealing his mules, and he had to prove he was a Mason to get them back. Although the jobs were plenty during the war, King did not bode well financially, getting paid with Confederate money, which ultimately proved worthless. Some say his descendants kept it through the 1920s and then threw it out with the trash.

His children joined him after the war in a family business, King Brothers Bridge Company. They rebuilt many of the southern bridges and many mills and railroads. In 1869, he was sixty-two and newly married to Sarah Jane

McManus. He turned much of the work over to his children and ran for the Alabama House of Representatives. He served two terms for Russell County and introduced several bills to improve the area and labor relief.

In the 1870s, he moved to LaGrange, Georgia, where he and his family continued to erect many of the buildings and educational facilities. He created a small colony for former slaves where they could study. He stayed in LaGrange until his death May 28, 1885. According to family members, King was carried "through the town and the men—and ladies too—came out of their shops and stores and stood with their arms folded over their hearts." He was buried just below the Confederate soldiers' area in Stonewall Jackson Cemetery in LaGrange.

It is unfortunate that this man who bridged and built much of the South is laid to rest based, clearly, on his color. While he stands apart from some of the unmarked graves there (he at least has a tombstone), it takes a moment to find his grave. Lonely and in solitude, his grave rests by the tree line. His son Marshall is buried beside a tree next to the creek bed a few feet away. His wives are both buried in Godwin Cemetery in Phenix City. It seems a sad ending to such an accomplished man.

While driving across many bridges in the area, you will find historical markers stating King built the first bridge here or there, but you won't find him in any major history books. If you ask any kid in middle school who Horace King is, most of them could not tell you. Our history books will tell you who invented the cotton gin; they will even tell you who created peanut butter. They will tell you about civil rights activists, and they will tell you about abolitionists. But they will not mention Horace King because, although you can walk through the Chattahoochee River area, throw a stone and hit one of King's accomplishments, much of what he had a part in is now in a slow state of demise. Perhaps it isn't just his architecture that is in peril but the memory of King altogether.

BIBLIOGRAPHY

Cherry, Francis L. *The History of Opelika and Her Agricultural Tributary Territory*. Opelika: Genealogical Society of East Alabama, 1996.

Davis, Jefferson. *The Rise and Fall of the Confederate Government*. New York: D. Appleton and Company, 1881.

Eggleston, George C. *Red Eagle and the Wars with the Greek Indians of Alabama*. New York: Dodd, Mead & Company, 1878.

French, T.L., Jr., and J.S. Lupold. *Bridging Deep South Rivers: The Life and Legend of Horace King*. Athens: University of Georgia Press, 2004.

Jones, James P. *Yankee Blitzkrieg: Wilson's Raid Through Alabama and Georgia*. Louisville: University Press of Kentucky, 2000.

LaFantasie, Glen W. *The Life and Lost Causes of Confederate Colonel William C. Oates*. New York: Oxford University Press, 2006.

Logue, Frank, and Victoria Logue. *Touring the Backroads of North and South Georgia*. Winston-Salem, NC: John F. Blair, 1997.

Mills, Charles. *Treasure Legends of the Civil War*. Alexandria, VA: Apple Cheeks Press, 2001.

Mooney, James. *History, Myths, and Sacred Formulas of the Cherokees*. Fairview, NC: Bright Mountain Books, Inc., 1992.

Pluckhahn, Thomas J. *Kolomoki: Settlement, Ceremony, and Status in the Deep South, A.D. 250–750*. Tuscaloosa: University of Alabama Press, 2003.

Potts, Eugenia D. *Historic Papers on the Causes of the Civil War*. Lexington, KY: Ashland Printing Co., 2006.

Sawyer, Gordon. *Northeast Georgia: A History*. Charleston, SC: Arcadia Publishing, Inc., 2001.

Serafin, F., M. Smith and J. Poe. *Haunted Auburn and Opelika*. Charleston, SC: The History Press, Haunted America, 2011.

Sherman, William T. *Memoirs of General Sherman*. New York: Literary Classics of the United States, Inc., 1990.

Trudeau, Noah A. *Southern Storm: Sherman's March to the Sea*. New York: HarperCollins, 2008.

Tuggle, William O. *Shem, Ham & Japheth (The Papers of W.O. Tuggle: Comprising His Indian Diary, Sketches, & Observations and Myths and Washington Journal in the Territory and at the Capital, 1879–1882*. Athens: University of Georgia Press, 1973.

Wortman, Marc. *The Bonfire: The Siege and Burning of Atlanta*. New York: Marc Wortman Public Affairs, 2009.

ONLINE SOURCES

Ancestry.com Operations, Inc. 2005. Miscellaneous records, Dale County, AL. Provo, UT: Original Data: Hayes, E.

Cashin, Edward. "Trustee Georgia, 1732–1752." *New Georgia Encyclopedia: History & Archaeology*. July 15, 2011. http://www.georgiaencyclopedia.org/nge/Article.jsp?id=h-816.

The Chaotic Order. "Old Town Cemetery." 2005. www.geocaching.com/ seek/cache_details.aspx?wp=GCRAJG.

"CSS *Jackson*: Largest Surviving Confederate Warship." Port Columbus, National Civil War Naval Museum. 2007. www.portcolumbus.org/ exhibits/css-jackson.

Daniels, G.C. "Kolomoki Mounds (500 AD)." Lost Worlds, February 17, 2011. www.lostworlds.org/kolomoki_mounds/3/.

Daniels, Margie. "Dale County Alabama Newspapers." Georgia and the Southeast Historical News. 1991. www.usgennet.org/usa/ga/topic/ news/dalenewspapers.htm.

Digital Library of Georgia. "Georgia Charter of 1732." Georgia Info. 2013. http://georgiainfo.galileo.usg.edu/charter.htm.

Federal Writers' Project. "Born in Slavery: Slave Narratives from the Federal Writers' Project, 1936–1938." Library of Congress Digital Collection. www.memory.loc.gov/ammem/snhtml/snhome.html.

French, T.L., and E.L. French. "Horace King, Bridge Builder." *Alabama Heritage* (Winter 1989): 34–47; online reprint, 2007. www.Alabamaheritage. com/vault/bridge.htm.

Ginger. "Huggin' Molly's and Abbeville's Vintage Goodness." Deep Fried Kudzu, April 22, 2011. http://www.deepfriedkudzu.com/2011/04/ huggin-mollys-and-abbevilles-vintage.html.

Howard. Miscellaneous records, Dale County, AL. Ozark, AL: unknown, 1973. www.Ancestry.com.

Knight, Professor Bernard. "Prince Madoc Myth or Legend?" Madoc International Research Association. www.madocresearch.net/ MoreInfo.html.

"The Legend of Trahlyta." Cherokee Gold. www.cherokeegold.net/ stonepilegap.html.

"Lost Treasures and Ghost Towns." About North Georgia. 1994. www. aboutnorthgeorgia.com/ang/Lost_Treasures_and_Ghost_Towns.

McLendon, N.G. "Abbeville Ghosts." Chattahoochee Heritage Project. 2012. www.chattahoocheeheritage.org/2012/04/abbeville-ghosts.

"The Nunnehi." Over-Hill Indian Nation (Cherokee Descendents). 1990. www.fl-wolf-clan.org/nunnehi.htm.

Pilcher, H. "The Science of Voodoo: When Mind Attacks Body." *New Scientist* no. 2708 (May 2009). www.newscientist.com/article/mg20227081.100-the-science-of-voodoo-when-mind-attacks-body.html?page=1.

The Professor. "Blood Mountain: Home to Unknown Creatures?" Georgia Mysteries, February 28, 2009. www.georgiamysteries.blogspot. com/2009/02/blood-mountain-home-to-unknown.html.

Pruitt, Paul McWhorter, Jr. "William Calvin Oates (1894–96)." *Encyclopedia of Alabama.* 2007. www.encyclopediaofalabama.org/face/Article. jsp?id=h-1410.

Serafin, Faith. "Springvilla Specters: Opelika, Alabama." Haunted Haven, October 24, 2012. www.hauntedhaven.blogspot.com/2012/10/ springvilla-specters.html.

Thornton, Richard. "The Nacoochee Mound: Site of the Nation's First Gold Rush, Part 1." *Examiner.com,* July 16, 2010. www.examiner.com/ article/the-nacoochee-mound-site-of-the-nation-s-first-gold-rush-part-1.

Tuggle, O.W. "The King of the Tie-Snakes." Sacred Texts. www.sacred-texts.com/nam/se/mtsi/mtsi030.htm.

Yisreal, Shearit. "Dothan: The Gateway to Salvation." 2010–2012. http:// www.shearit.net/Articles/BrickP/Dothan.pdf.

Yronwode, Catherine. "Hoodoo, Conjure, and Rootwork: African American Folk Magic." 1995–2000. http://www.luckymojo.com/ hoodoohistory.html.

ABOUT THE AUTHOR

Michelle Smith is a resident of Auburn, Alabama, and a graduate of Auburn University with a bachelor's of arts in criminal justice and criminology. Michelle is a dedicated historic researcher and an investigator for the Alabama Paranormal Research Team. Michelle has previously published the book *Haunted Auburn and Opelika* (The History Press, 2011). She also writes a blog, Southern Belle's History, which covers historical true-crime pieces as well as haunted sites and their historical significance. Her fields of interest include Native American folklore and symbolism; southern folklore; American history, particularly military history and especially the Civil War; abnormal psychology and true crime; and paranormal research and historic locations. Michelle believes historical preservation is a must. She takes it as a challenge to separate the truth from the bias and believes it her duty to pass on history in its purest form to future generations.

Visit us at
www.historypress.net
....

This title is also available as an e-book